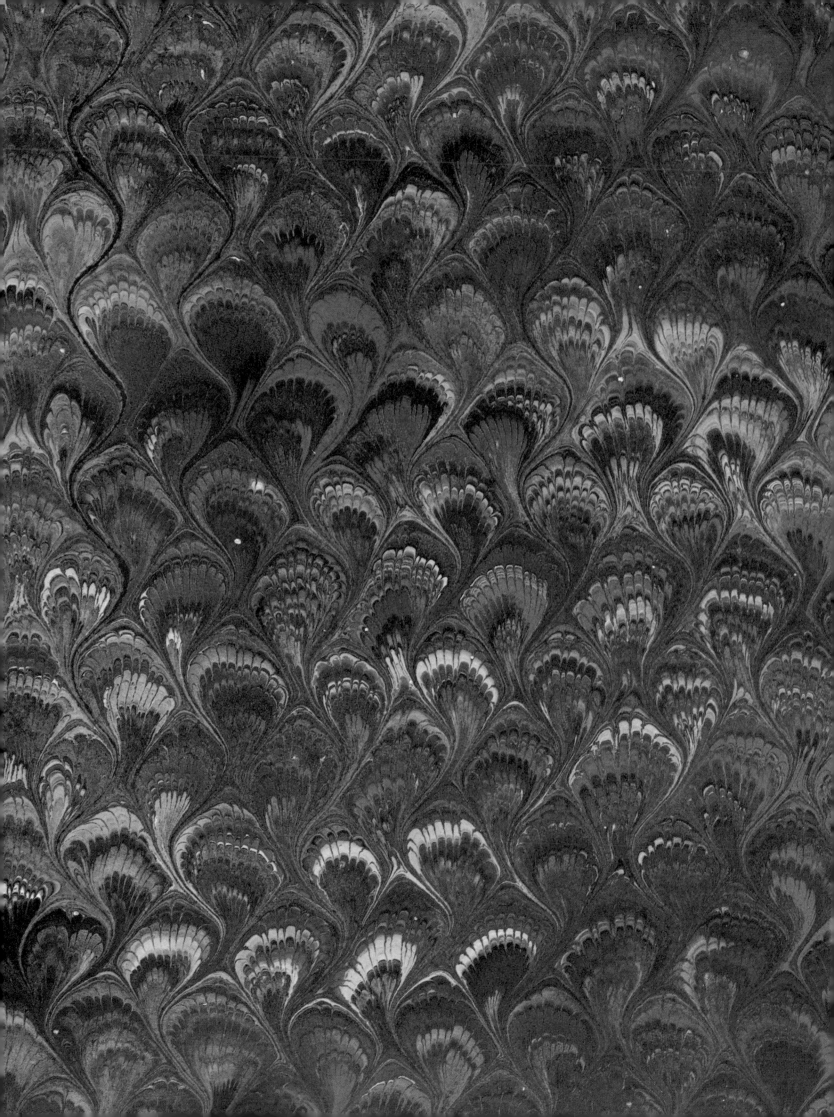

AN INTRODUCTION TO

Heraldry

AN INTRODUCTION TO

Heraldry

STEFAN OLIVER

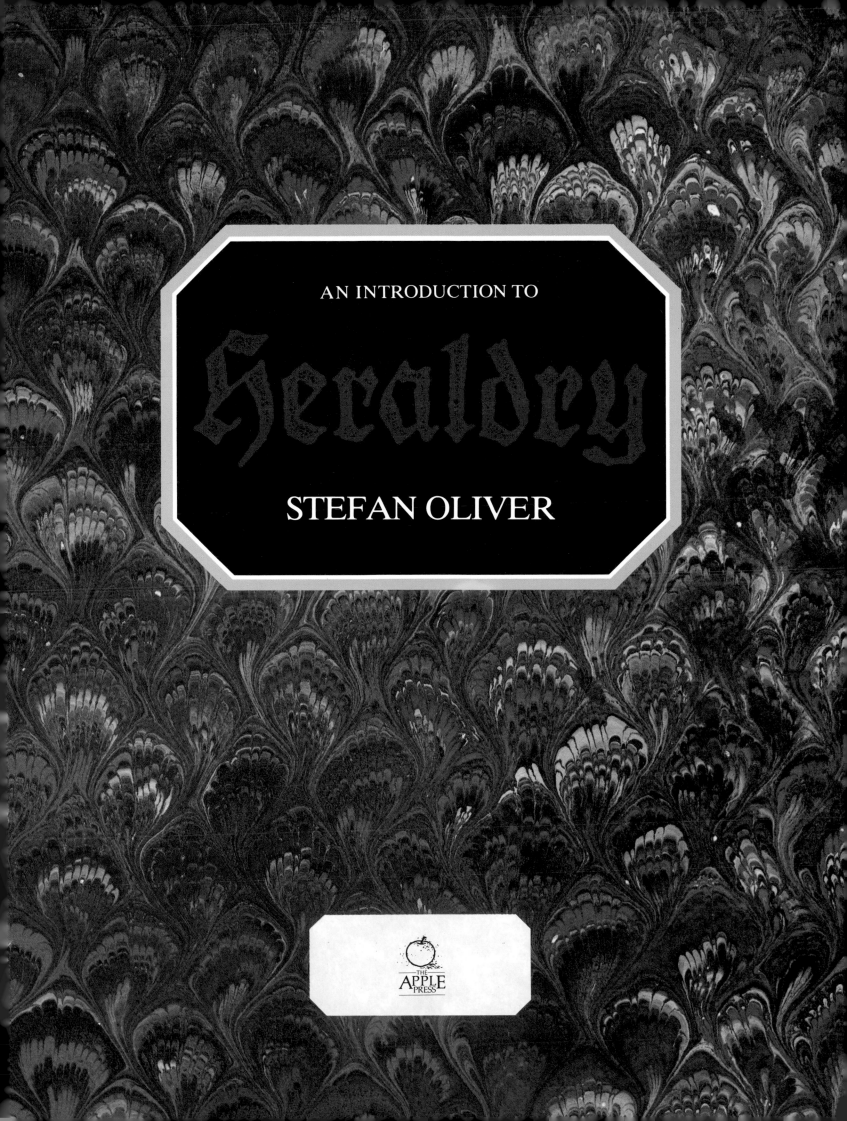

THE
APPLE
PRESS

A QUINTET BOOK

Published by The Apple Press
6 Blundell Street
London N7 9BH

Reprinted 1991

ISBN 1–85076–097–7

This book was designed and produced by
Quintet Publishing Limited
6 Blundell Street
London N7

Art Director: Peter Bridgewater
Designer: Linda Moore
Editors: Robert Stewart, Shaun Barrington
Illustrator: Stefan Oliver

Typeset in Great Britain by
Central Southern Typesetters, Eastbourne
Manufactured in Hong Kong by Regent
Publishing Services Limited
Printed in Hong Kong by Leefung-Asco
Printers Limited

Contents

Introduction

EW PEOPLE can fail to be impressed by the eye-catching display of Heraldic insignia. The magnificence of their colourful array is seen all around us, on public buildings, in churches, on flags, on documents and advertizing materials, on tee-shirts and vehicles — in fact adorning everyday items of all kinds. They provide a decorative and attractive display and a permanent symbol of ownership and individuality in a unique and ever-lasting way and carry the ancient traditions of chivalry, honour and duty into the nuclear age.

In this age of mass production and computerised conformity we are all subject to the powerful influences of television and advertising. The production of consumer items is in the hands of fewer and fewer, bigger and bigger international corporations. The clothes and cars that we buy, the houses in which we live and the foods that we eat, are becoming more and more the same.

People are becoming increasingly interested in finding ways, no matter how small, to assert their own personalities. Heraldry is able to offer people a symbol that is legally personal to them, one which they can pass on to their descendants, which may be used in a great variety of ways to decorate their property in a dignified fashion and which carries historical links into modern times.

People are beginning to understand that Heraldry is not simply a subject of medieval his-

tory, but is as alive and meaningful today as it has ever been. Unhappily, misconceptions about Heraldry — many of them deliberately sustained by people who wish to wrap the subject in mystery — have tended to confuse people and put them off the subject entirely. People fear and deride things that they do not understand. Heraldry, being an ancient subject, has customs and a language which are unfamiliar to us and which tend to confuse and hide its true meaning. It is versed in an ancient, though simple and fairly limited, terminology that tends to mystify those who are unwilling to learn it. People are, however, beginning to accept technical jargons as they become more widely used in industry and technology, so that this barrier is happily being rapidly removed.

There is, unfortunately, a quite unjustified social resistance to Heraldry, fostered by those who do not understand the subject. The origins of Heraldry lay in the desire for personal identification. It is true that in medieval times the people who sought this identification were of a high rank in society and that Heraldry became an honour. It is true, too, that it has remained a mark of honour down to our own day. One of the great strengths of our society, however, is that this honour is not confined to a handful of people born into privilege, but is available to anyone who by his own effort or good fortune has been able to take the steps needed to become a 'top person'. There are those who feel that an honour should not be inherited by succeeding generations. But who, having earned for himself an honour, or a fortune, would not leave it to his children? The proposition that anyone in this position would divest himself of everything and tell his children to start from the beginning, as he did, is preposterous. Let those who complain about the unfairness of inherited wealth or honour set about obtaining for themselves that which they purport to despise. Let also, however, those who have inherited an honour, be it an Heraldic device or an ancient title, remember that they are the living representatives of the one to whom the honour was originally granted and that it is their duty to preserve and foster its worth.

At first sight, a large Achievement of Arms, dazzling though it may be in its brilliant colours and array, presents an incomprehensible mass of fine detail that is bewildering to the uninitiated. And if they look up the Achievement in a book, they may be baffled by what they read and left with more questions than answers. What is it all about? Where did it all come from? Why is it so apparently incomprehensible?

This short book cannot unravel all the detail that has accumulated over many centuries; nor can it provide all the answers; the hope is that it will start readers along the path that will lead to a more scholarly and comprehensive study, once their enthusiasm has been kindled and their curiosity rewarded with a preliminary understanding.

The tomb of the Countess of Hertford in Westminster Abbey.

CHAPTER ONE

The Origins of Heraldry

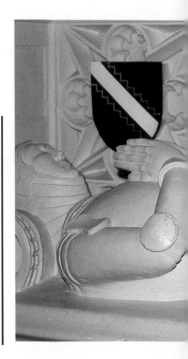

Heraldry has its origins in warfare and stems from the warrior's primitive desire to display an emblem in battle to strengthen his own morale and strike terror into the heart of his enemy. All over the world and all through history examples of this kind of decoration can be found. As soon as man was able to grasp the advantage to be had from using a weapon to hit or pierce his foe, he had also to develop a shield to protect him from retaliation. The large surface thus provided was the ideal vehicle for military decoration. Those early devices were not thought to be hereditary and so they were, really, pre-Heraldic. It is doubtful whether those devices were permanent; and a person may have used different ones on different occasions. It is known, for example, that the Norman knights did not later use the devices with which, if the evidence of the Bayeux tapestry is accurate, they fought at Hastings. By then, however, it was already necessary, because of armour in the form of chain mail and helmets that covered a large part of the face, for leaders and knights to have devices on their shields, flags and standards by which they could be recognized.

The great feudal overlords also found it desirable to have some form of recognizable symbol with which they could authenticate documents and instructions that they issued to their largely illiterate subjects; and so there came into use seals that depicted the overlord on his horse, in battle array, with a shield bearing his devices.

Church establishments also used seals, with a picture of the bishop or abbot, as appropriate, engraved upon them. All the land in Europe was nominally in the hands of kings, who rewarded their followers by giving them land. For the most part kings were wise enough not to give large, single blocks of land to anybody, thus diminishing the risk of powerful territorial magnates setting themselves up as rivals to the throne. Landowners usually held their estates in scattered parcels, and since they were unable to make frequent visits to all of them, the need for seals was greatly increased. Seals, carried by the lords' messengers, were marks of authority, badges of identification.

KNIGHT FEES

Landowners held their land on the condition that they provide knights to ride to battle when the king required them. This was known as 'knight fee'. Only very wealthy landowners could supply a sufficient number of knights from their own resources and so they, in turn,

would grant some of their land to lesser knights in return for knight fee to ride for the king or for themselves, as required. The more land one acquired, the greater one's power and influence and the more knights one could put at one's own or the king's service.

In the recurrent feudal wars of the time, when knights rode all over the country to fight on one side or another, it was necessary that each of them should wear a badge or symbol of the lord to whom he belonged and on whose side he was fighting. Thus kings and lords adopted some simple object as a badge to distinguish their followers in the field. This practice gained wide acceptance in western Europe, during the Crusades of the 11th, 12th and 13th

ABOVE RIGHT The tomb of Sir William Clopton, son of Sir Thomas Clopton, displaying (LEFT TO RIGHT) his paternal arms, the arms of his mother Elizabeth Mylde, and his own arms joined on the same shield with his first wife Marjory (daughter of Sir Robert Drury of Suffolk), and his second wife, also Marjory (daughter of Elias Francis of Suffolk).

RIGHT Detail of the Bayeux Tapestry depicting the Battle of Hastings between King Harold of England and the invading forces of Duke William of Normandy. The devices that the figures display are not thought to be heraldic because the same figures wear different emblems in different episodes shown in the tapestry, and the descendants of those same individuals did not display the same emblems.

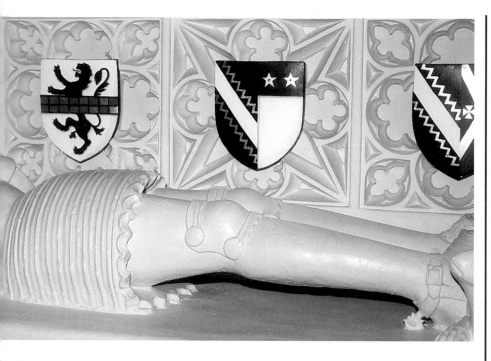

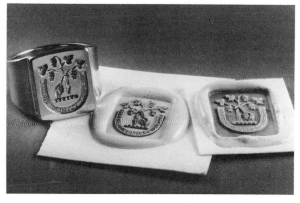

ABOVE *A pruning hook on a crest, on a specially commissioned seal-engraved signet ring; (engraver, Clare Street). The latin motto translates as 'Virtue flourishes by her wound'. Such mottos are not uniquely held: seven families have in fact adopted this example.*

centuries. The Holy Land, the birthplace of Christianity, was overrun by the Muslim Turks, who cut off Christians' access to it. The Pope called on all Christian leaders to take up arms and liberate the Holy Lands. Numerous expeditions were mounted from western Europe, some successful, some not (and some bizarre in the extreme). Men set forth under the sign of the Cross, emblazoned on their cloaks, shields and banners, in different colours and different forms for each country and large group. Their swords were made in the shape of crosses and engraved with pious emblems and inscriptions. Thus the idea of a collective badge to identify a group took universal hold throughout Europe.

ACCUMULATION OF LAND

Any ambitious lord sought to increase the amount of his land. One of the best ways was to marry a lady who held land in her own right, either because she was a widow or because she was her father's heiress. As the number of young men who died in battle or from disease was high, and the number of wives who died in childbirth considerable, there was ample opportunity by judicious marriages to acquire large estates. A new husband would mark his authority over newly acquired lands by displaying on his seal the armorial bearings of this new land. This practice meant that the mounted figure on the seals was soon dropped in favour of one shield showing all the arms belonging to the different people who had formerly held the land. Some seals also had the main arms engraved on a shield in the middle and the new ones on smaller shields around the outside. The passing of arms from one person to another in this way inevitably led to their being passed from father to son. So Heraldry, as we know it today, was born.

THE IDEALS OF CHIVALRY

In medieval times land was farmed by people who paid a rent in kind, either as part of their crop or in service to their lord, who was thus free to devote himself to other pursuits. Much of his energy was devoted to military activities, either on his own behalf or on that of his overlord or king. With the example of the Crusades before them, young men prepared themselves by prayer, fasting and ritual to join a company of knights and to lead a life in the military service of others. So the high ideals of courage, perseverance and generosity to others were bred into them at an early age. In order to acquire skill in battle, they spent many hours in practice combat. This led to friendly competitions and the idea of the tournament was born. Knights from all over Europe went from one tournament to the next, trying their skill, displaying their prowess and winning such prizes and favour as they could. Tournaments were great social events and therefore occasions for brilliant and exaggerated Heraldic display. The contestants hung their shields up outside their lodgings when they arrived so that everyone would know who was in town. People came from miles around to see the spectacle and visit the accompanying fair. On the day of the tournament itself, the contestants displayed their armorial bearings on their shields, their Coats of Arms and their horse trappings; they painted them on tents and marquees, on banners and flags, on anything that they could find to make a splendid display. They fashioned on their helmets, from wood or softened leather, ornate crests representing animals and birds and all kinds of devices. Their shields were carried around the arena, for all to see, by pages dressed in costumes of exotic and fierce animals. The spectators and their wives wore their armorial bearings emblazoned on their cloaks, dresses and surcoats. The whole event was a stunning pageant and carnival. The proceedings were presided over by the Heralds, who acted as masters of ceremonies and referees and ensured that things ran smoothly.

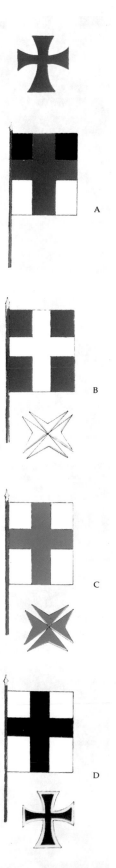

LEFT *Elizabeth Talbot* (LEFT), *daughter of John Talbot, Earl of Shrewsbury and wife of John de Mowbray, the last Mowbray Duke of Norfolk, and Elizabeth Tilney* (RIGHT), *daughter of Sir Francis Tilney and wife of Thomas Howard, Duke of Norfolk; each displays her own arms on her dress and her husband's arms on her cloak.*

A

B

C

D

The banners and badges of four orders of crusader knights are illustrated here: A Templars B Hospitalers C St Lazarus D Teutonic order.

ABOVE Detail from a military roll compiled in 1448; a jousting tournament.

RIGHT Sir William Clopton, son of Sir Thomas Clopton; the ermine spot on the arms he displays on his surcoat distinguishes him from his father.

FAR RIGHT Ann Denston, in Long Melford Church, Suffolk; she wears her own arms on her dress and those of her husband on her cloak.

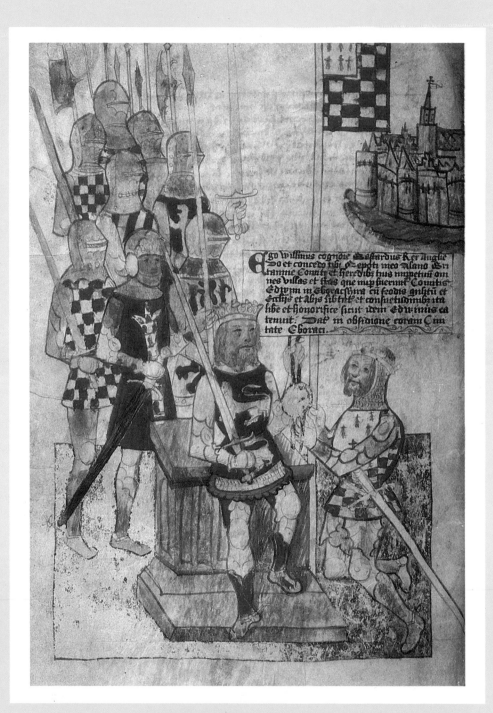

*The Duke of Normandy, now William the Conqueror,
granting land in England to his supporters, who are
depicted bearing the arms later attributed to them.*

CHAPTER TWO

The Heralds

HERALDS have been employed by kings and large landowners, principally as messengers and ambassadors, from very early times. They are believed to have come originally from the ranks of roaming troubadours and minstrels, who went from one place to another with their songs and tales. It seems clear that when they were acting as messengers or ambassadors Heralds were free to come and go as they pleased, even across national frontiers. They wore a tabard emblazoned with their master's arms while on 'official duty' and this was supposed to guarantee them protection. An attack on a Herald who was wearing his master's arms was equivalent to an attack on the master. As had been pointed out earlier most lords had land scattered about the country. Heralds were, therefore, constantly travelling and meeting other Heralds and other lords; and in this way they soon began to gather considerable knowledge of the armorial bearings of other people. This gave rise to their second important function, that of staff officer in battle.

BELOW The funeral procession of Queen Elizabeth of England; the heralds are in full funereal black, with their sovereign arms displayed on their tabards.

FAR RIGHT A roll of arms of the Lord of the Manor of Long Melford Hall in Suffolk, dating from 1044.

THE HERALD'S ROLE AS STAFF OFFICER

In medieval times many disputes were settled by force. Before embarking upon a dispute over borders with your neighbour, however, it was important to know how many knights he could put in the field against you. Heralds could easily discover this. During a battle itself they were also able to tell their lord, by recognizing the arms, who the opponents were, how many knights they could put into the field and what men they had under their command. They also reported who had left or joined the battle and what forces they had taken away or added. This last function was very important, since many of the combatants were involved only for what they could obtain for themselves; expected allies sometimes held back from the fray and joined it only when it was clear which side was going to win — not always the side with whom they had started out!

Heralds quite often had to decide who had won a battle. At the battle of Agincourt the French and English Heralds watched the day's events together and in the evening reported to King Henry of England that the 'day was his'.

Another important function was the identifying of captives. Important people were held hostage for the ransom that could be gained and ordinary people were put to death. It was obviously necessary to get this right! Heralds also had the unenviable task of identifying the dead. This presented no great difficulty when men

THE CORPES

Mr Richard Browne, Esquire   Mr Richard Leenor, Esquire   Rugecrosse.   Eight gentlemen for the Corpes

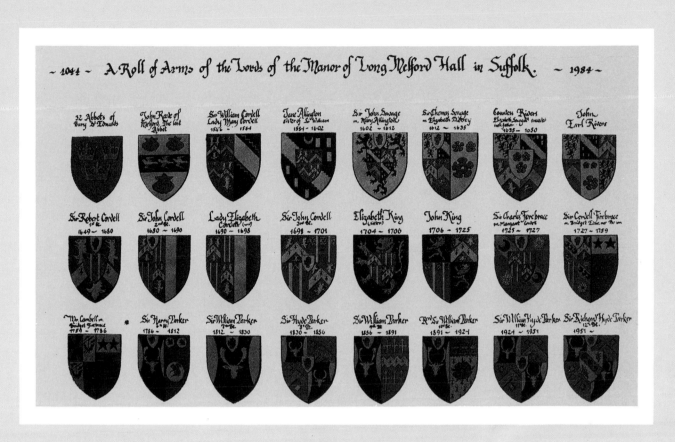

~1044~ A Roll of Arms of the Lords of the Manor of Long Melford Hall in Suffolk. ~1984~

Percullis   Rugedragon   Mr Dallender and
Mr Laurence Staughton} Esquires

fought largely on foot and wore chain mail with open helmets made of iron. The slain could be easily recognized. Knights used to wear over their chain mail a long, loose, padded coat, made of tough material, to help protect them from sword cuts and they adopted the practice of painting their armorial bearings on these. This was called coat armour, or coat of arms, and is the derivation of the phrase, Coat of Arms. If the face of the slain was not recognizable, it was possible to identify him by his Coat of Arms. When, in later years, knights started to wear plate armour and closed helmets, it was impossible to recognize anyone except by his Coat of Arms; the Heralds therefore insisted that knights continue to wear a short surcoat, with their arms painted on them, so that mistakes could be avoided.

When knights charged into battle on their great war horses, wielding huge axes, lances and swords, the force of the impact must have been terrible. Not only was it a question of identifying the dead, but a matter of finding all the right pieces! The use of arms emblazoned on everything, including the crest of the helmet, enabled the Heralds to perform this grisly task. The clash of a couple of hundred knights, charging full pelt at one another and wielding every

ABOVE A 15th century illustration of the Battle of Agincourt (1415); only the more important figures in the painting are depicted wearing surcoats. The lives of those French nobles thus identified would have been spared after the battle, and ransomed.

matters and they began to keep lists of all the armorial bearings used at different tournaments, gatherings and battles and of the people who bore them. These lists were collected on long rolls of parchment and were called Rolls of Arms, or simply Rolls. Many of these have survived and they provide a valuable record of early Heraldry. Because the Heralds became so involved in the study and recording of Coats of Arms and in advising and adjudicating on matters relating to them, the business became known as Heraldry. In England the Heralds were incorporated by royal charter in 1484. Since people continued to assume Coats of Arms, without having them registered and recorded at the College, disputes frequently arose over who was the actual owner of a Coat of Arms. Consequently, the Heralds were required to tour the country and record all Coats of Arms, so that they could be registered and disputes be settled. Most of these visitations, as they were called, took place in the 16th century. They form the basis upon which ownership of arms is proved today. The records, however, are not complete, for those were stormy times in England, and in some instances people were unable to answer the call of the visiting Herald, because they were confined to their place of residence. The motive of the Visitation may often have been political and not strictly for the well-being of heraldry. It was a worthwhile exercise for sovereigns to record their supporters and disqualify those who could not support them.

THE ROLE OF THE HERALDS TODAY

Heralds still have important duties as officers of the Crown, and apart from these duties are very active in Heraldic affairs. Interest in Heraldic matters is steadily increasing and there are now more matters needing their attention than ever before. Their work falls into three categories.

Confirming arms There are still people eager to have confirmed to them arms that they have always used, but for which they have to prove a right of descent. The Heralds are glad to help in this work, which involves a lot of patient genealogical research, since, despite the records of centuries, a mass of detail still needs to be recorded.

Granting arms Any worthy person may apply for a grant of arms and the Heralds will be pleased to steer the applicant safely through the problems. The steps are roughly these. It is necessary, first of all, to check that an aspirant armiger is not entitled to an existing Coat of Arms. If he is not, it is then necessary to consider with him a possible design and to check that it is not already held by someone. Once this is established and the design is approved by all parties it can be granted to the applicant as the sole right of him and his legal descendants. As well as private individuals, many commercial undertakings and corporate institutions apply

kind of dismembering weapon, must have been sheer bedlam. No wonder so many knight effigies are shown wearing armour! It was probably so battered that it could not be removed.

HERALDS AND TOURNAMENTS

Because of their knowledge of armorial bearings, Heralds were required to recognize and announce contestants at tournaments and it soon became their responsibility to organize and referee these events. Because of the social nature of the event and the desire by everyone to put on a good display, Heralds were necessary to advise would-be contestants about the choice of armorial bearings that they could use. They were able to make sure that no one chose the arms of another, already in use.

People came to them for advice on Heraldic

for grants of arms.

Devising arms The Heralds of Great Britain have jurisdiction only over subjects of the crown. Although many people of British origin who are citizens of other countries wish to register Coats of Arms or varieties of arms belonging to their families to show their ancient lineage, the Heralds cannot grant arms to them. They can, however, following the proper searches, 'devise' arms that could be used and register them in their records so that they will not be issued to others.

The Heralds take great care to ensure that any arms, crests, supporters, mottos, badges or standards are unique to the grantees. This is the point of the exercise. Heraldry exists to identify individuals. There is no such thing as 'Arms of a Name'. The notion that such a thing exists is a deliberate misconception perpetrated by those who would exploit the ignorant for base profit. Knowledge of the outlines of Heraldry protects people from being persuaded to buy a shield of arms with their name on it, on the false understanding that it might be theirs.

THE LANGUAGE OF HERALDRY

One of the things that puts people off a study of Heraldry is the language. They come up against terms which they simply do not understand. Like many specialist subjects, Heraldry has its own technical language, or jargon, that must be learned. As modern life becomes more and more technical specialist jargons are entering more and more into everyday life; as a result people are showing less resistance to the jargon of Heraldry than they once did. In this way the circumstances of modern life are removing an obstacle to the study of what is, after all, a medieval science.

Heraldry had its origins in western Europe at a time when the predominant language was Norman French and some of that language survives in the Heraldic terms employed today. There are not, however, very many such terms surviving; those that do, chiefly concern the basic matters of design and colour. The simplest way to learn them is to use them; so they will be gradually introduced throughout this book and explained as they appear. One source of endless confusion, however, which must be mastered at the outset, is the question of left and and right.

LEFT AND RIGHT

Right, called 'dexter', and left, called 'sinister', apply from the point of view of the person carrying, or standing behind, the shield. So 'dexter' means his right as he stands opposite you and you look at him. Similarly, 'sinister' means his left. The dexter, or righthand side of the bearer, is thought to be the most noble, and most Heraldic emblems are drawn facing that way. It is only if they face in another direction that any comment, or explanation, is required.

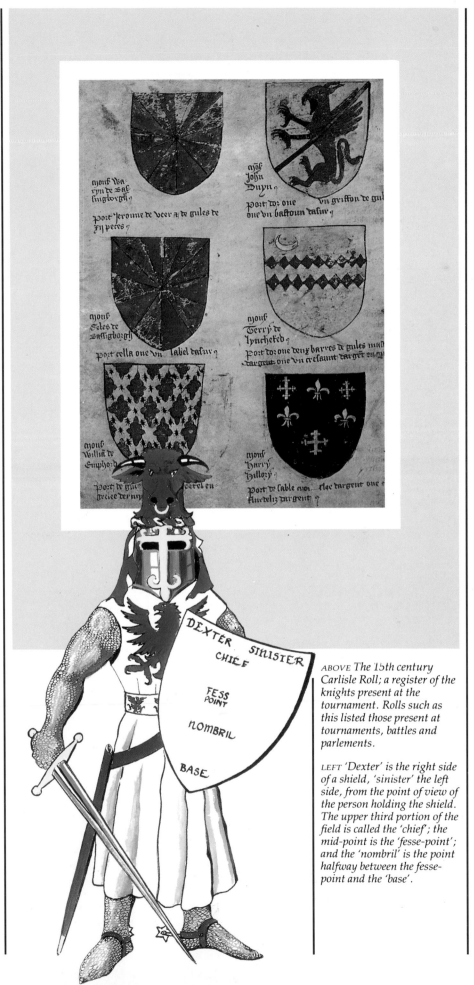

ABOVE *The 15th century Carlisle Roll; a register of the knights present at the tournament. Rolls such as this listed those present at tournaments, battles and parlements.*

LEFT *'Dexter' is the right side of a shield, 'sinister' the left side, from the point of view of the person holding the shield. The upper third portion of the field is called the 'chief'; the mid-point is the 'fesse-point'; and the 'nombril' is the point halfway between the fesse-point and the 'base'.*

CHAPTER THREE

The Colours of Heraldry

*E*VEN THE most casual observer may be struck with delight by a bold and colourful heraldic display and it is important from the outset to discuss the Heraldic colours and the ways in which they are used.

The student will soon become aware that the colours of Heraldry are in fact few; it is by skilful combinations of them that bold effects are produced. The colours, or tinctures, as they are properly called, must always be of the clearest and purest tone possible to give a bold, brilliant and unambiguous effect. They were originally chosen so that the wearer would be readily identifiable at a distance, and in the 'pell-mell' of battle, and their bold and striking combination is a vital part of the continuing tradition.

The tinctures fall into three groups: (1) those that represent metals; (2) those that represent colours; and (3) those that represent furs.

THOSE THAT REPRESENT METAL

The tincture white represents silver and is called 'argent', abbreviated 'ar'. The tincture yellow represents gold and is called 'or'.

It is quite proper to use silver or gold paint, but because of the difficulty of finding suitable pigments that will not blacken with age, it has become the custom to paint these tinctures with yellow and white. In very important documents it is customary to use gold or silver leaf on those parts that should be of these colours.

THOSE THAT REPRESENT COLOURS

These are listed below, each with its Heraldic term and usual abbreviation. When a Coat of Arms is drawn in black and white, it is necessary to indicate what the tinctures are; a scheme of shading to use for each tincture (which is also shown), has therefore been developed.

There was at one time a custom of describing the colours used by the planets and precious stones and metals. Because examples of this practice may still be found, they are set out in the table below. The colours are red, blue, green, black and purple.

There have been introduced in more recent times the following shades, or stains, as they are called — orange, blood red, mulberry purple and sky blue. Their use is not widespread, although sky blue, as opposed to the true royal blue normally used, is being introduced especially by people connected with aviation and space exploration.

Many designs, of which a number are shown here, have been devised to represent ermine in Heraldry. Each is a representation of the animal's tail.

THOSE THAT REPRESENT FURS

Because of the importance of fur and its common use in contemporary dress, colours and patterns have been devised to represent fur in Heraldry. The use of fur in a variety of forms is common in Heraldry, though it does not necessarily indicate any special rank.

Ermine The fur most commonly found is ermine, in its several forms. In northern climates the common stoat, a fierce, small, predatory animal, normally coloured a sandy chestnut, changes its coat to pure white in the winter, but for the tip of the tail, which remains black. Ermine furs were highly prized and, because of their relative rarity and because of the large number of them needed, for example, to line a royal cloak, they were extremely expensive. They were sewn together, still with the tail attached, which hung loose. The Heraldic representation of ermine is white, strewn with a regular black pattern representing the tails. A large number of designs have been recorded in Heraldic representation of these tails.

Various combinations are also used, each with its own name:

ERMINE White with black tails
ERMINOIS Gold with black tails
ERMINES Black with white tails
PEAN Black with gold tails

Vair (or Vaire, Vairy, Verre, Verrey, Verry) The next most common fur is vair, in a variety of forms. It is always drawn as an alternating pattern of rounded or angular pieces of different colours. It is said by contemporary writers to represent the skins of the grey squirrel, sewn belly to back alternately, thus producing the white and blue pattern. Vair is always blue and white, unless other colours are specified, in which case the first colour mentioned is always the piece in the top dexter corner. Vair is met in a variety of forms and these are shown below. A vair pattern of colours other than blue and white is always described as being 'vairy of' whatever the colours specified. The most common forms of vair are vair, counter-vair, potent, counter-potent, vair ancient, and vary.

DIAPERING

When the Christian knights returned from the Crusades they brought back with them fantastic brocades, woven materials and silks that they discovered in the sophisticated and civilized (compared to their own more robust environment) society that they encountered around the shores of the eastern Mediterranean. Cere-

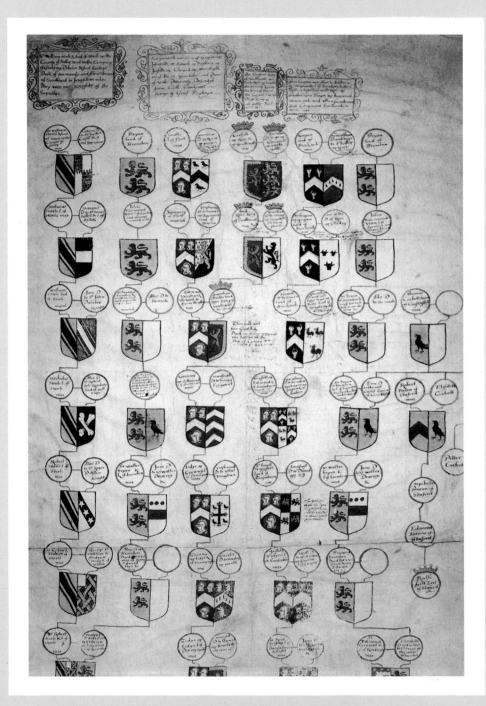

The 16th century armorial family tree of Anne Hale;
note the use of the colours yellow and white in place of
gold and silver.

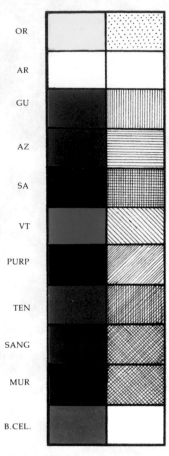

This chart shows the
colours of Heraldry, each
with the abbreviation of
its name.

monial Coats of Arms and banners and flags were made of these new exotic materials. Diapering is an attempt to repeat these fantastic patterns, as decorative treatment, on a painted shield, without diminishing the true colour. It was usually carried out in a different shade of the same colour or in painted gold. The patterns usually have an abstract swirl or leaf motif, though there are many examples in which geometric designs or very small, repeated Heraldic devices were used.

THE RULES CONCERNING THE USE OF COLOUR

There are not many rules, as such, in Heraldry, and by far the most important of them concern the use of colour. For the sake of visual clarity and artistic harmony, these few rules must be observed.

◆ *Never* place a metal on a metal, e.g. a gold lion on a silver shield.

◆ *Never* place a colour on a colour, e.g. a red lion on a blue shield.

◆ *Always* place a metal on a colour or a colour on a metal, e.g. a gold lion on a red, blue, green or black shield, or a red, blue, green or black lion on a silver or gold shield.

◆ A fur can take the place of a metal or a colour.

All good rules exist to be broken. There are plenty of examples of this in Heraldry. They merely strengthen the need for the rules, which developed in the Middle Ages, and still endure today, long after Heraldry's practical use has disappeared. That the rules have survived more or less intact until now must be some kind of proof of their worth.

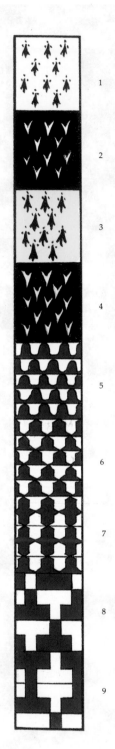

This chart shows the
various combinations
representing the tinctures
of the two most common
furs in Heraldry, ermine
and vair.

1 Ermine 2 Ermines
3 Erminois 4 Pean 5 Vair
Ancient 6 Vair 7 Counter-
Vair 8 Potent 9 Counter-
Potent

THE COLOURS OF HERALDRY						
Colour	Heraldic Term	Abbreviation	Metal	Precious Stone	Planet	Zodiac Sign
Gold	Or	or	Gold	Topaz	Sun	Leo
Silver	Argent	ar	Silver	Pearl	Moon	Cancer
Red	Gules	gu	Iron	Ruby	Mars	Aries
Blue	Azure	az or B	Tin	Sapphire	Jupiter	Taurus
Black	Sable	sa	Lead	Diamond	Saturn	Capricorn
Green	Vert or Sinople	vt	Copper	Emerald	Venus	Gemini
Purple	Purpure	purp	Quicksilver	Amethyst	Mercury	Sagittarius
Orange	Tenné	ten				
Blood	Sanguine	sang				
Mulberry	Murrey	mur				
Sky blue	Bleu céleste	B.cel.				

CHAPTER FOUR
Heraldic Accessories

*I*T HAS been shown thus far that Heraldic devices were originally used to identify individuals in the press of battle or to authenticate documents and instructions by way of seals. These devices were painted on the shield, on to the Coat of Arms, onto the horse trappings, on flags, banners and tents and used in every way possible to identify the wearer and owner. With the invention of guns in the 14th century, armour slowly began to fall into disuse, since it was no longer possible for a man both to be mobile and to wear armour sufficiently strong to stop bullet and ball. It therefore ceased to be difficult to identify men on the battlefield and heraldic insignia ceased to be used for this practical purpose by the 17th century. They have continued to be used however, as an artistic and traditional way to identify a person; and shields, though they no longer serve a protective function, have remained the chief vehicle upon which to display armorial insignia.

Armorial insignia are commonly depicted on other accessories and devices besides the shield. The whole assemblage is known as 'the Achievement', which is the correct term to describe the total collection of a person's Heraldic accessories, also called appurtenances. Different countries and customs dictate that Achievements contain different items. This chapter describes the parts of an Achievement.

THE SHIELD

The shield is the principal vehicle for the display of armorial insignia and is the only essential ingredient in an Achievement of Arms. The devices on the shield are the individual insignia — the armorial bearings — that mark one man from another (See Chap 5). The shield is found in a variety of shapes and these are the outcome of different usages, fashions and times. The principal shapes and styles are shown below.

The long shield, which gives the most protection, was used when men fought on foot. It afforded a protection against arrows, as well as in closer combat.

The short or heater-shaped shield, which was especially devised for use in tournaments, was strong enough to withstand a hit with a lance. Its shape provided the most protection and deflected the lance from the bearer. It was also called the 'target', or 'targ', after the point at which a knight aimed in a charge at a tournament.

The square-shaped shield became more popular when the custom developed of displaying more than one set of armorial bearings on one shield.

The horsehead shield is so called because its shape is thought to have developed from the armour plate used to protect the head and face of a knight's horse. It was quite often used by ecclesiastical dignitaries when the military-style shield was felt to be inappropriate.

The lozenge and oval Armigerous women customarily display their arms on an oval or a lozenge, since it has always been felt that it is inappropriate for a woman to display arms on a 'military' shield.

Ornamental cartouches and other shapes Once the practical use of the shield disappeared, arms began to be displayed on all kinds of ornamental shapes and designs of a perplexing

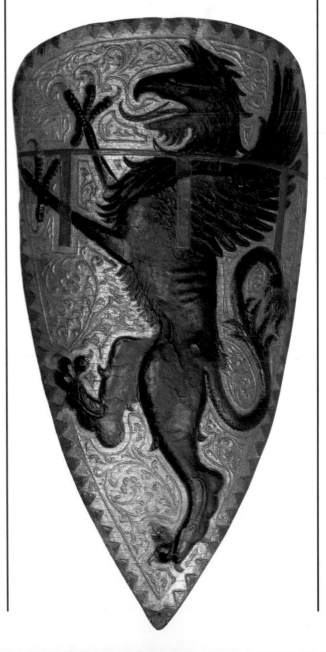

RIGHT A ceremonial shield of 15th century Florentine workmanship; note the diapering on the gold background.

*The achievement of arms of the Drury family,
displayed on a stained glass cartouche for hanging in a window.*

A

B

C

C

D

E

The principal shapes and
styles of shields are as
follows: **A** the long shield
B the short or heater-
shaped shield **C** the
square-shaped shield
(shown in two styles) **D**
the horsehead shield, and
E the lozenge.

variety. Nowadays there has been something of a return to the beginnings of Heraldry, to an earlier, simple style, and a simple shield is now fashionable. The square-shaped shield is used when several different armorial bearings are represented; the oval and the lozenge are still used to display women's Heraldic devices. But it should be made clear that the shape of the shield is not sacred; it can be changed, due consideration being given to style and period, to any shape that best suits the design of the armorial bearings that it displays or the article upon which it is placed. All that matters is that the design conforms to Heraldic ideals and be in good taste.

THE HELMET

In the days of hand-to-hand warfare adequate protection for the head was provided by a simple iron cap or basinet, which was sufficient to protect the wearer from sword blows. Later a noseplate and cheek plates were added. When cavalry was introduced the helmet had to be much stronger and so the helmet which closed with a visor and which had a plate around the neck — a gorget — was introduced. Helmets with bars and grids across the face were also introduced.

Ceremonial helmets, usually of the type with bars, were made of softened leather and were richly decorated. They were used as vehicles to display the crest, especially in countries where whole families display the same armorial bearings on the shield and identify the individual only by a different crest.

In some countries it is the custom to use dif-ferent types and posture of helmet, or 'helm' as it is more usually called, to diffentiate men according to this social rank. This, however, is only a custom, not a rule, and it is often broken.

The pot helm This, the oldest type of helm, was worn over the top of the small basinet and chain-mail gorget. Its use in Heraldry is limited to gentlemen in Scotland and some families of ancient lineage, in Germany and Denmark.

The tilting helm This helm was used by gentlemen and esquires in England, the Scandinavian countries, Germany and Poland, and (though less commonly), by persons of all ranks throughout Europe. Some members of the German, Austrian, Hungarian and Polish nobility have used it to show that their armorial bearings are of more ancient lineage than those depicted by 'newer men' on the more modern barred helm. It is also used in Italian Heraldry for non-titled ranks. Civic and corporate armorial bearings in England usually use this type of helm.

The helm with open visor and no bars This type is used, usually facing the front, by British knights and baronets (hereditary knights) and Russian Leibkanpanez.

The barred helm This helm, found in a variety of forms and styles, is used all over Europe, usually to denote titled rank, though in Belgium, the Netherlands and Spain it is used by untitled ranks as well. The posture of the helm varies from country to country, and alterations in the number of bars and the artistic treatment are then used to signify distinctions of rank. An English peer of whatever rank, for example, uses a five-barred helm facing to the left (as you look at it). On the Continent this helm, whether facing the front or either side, is used by all ranks. In Italy and Spain the posture, the number of bars and the amount of gold used demonstrate the rank of the bearer. In Denmark and the Netherlands a silver helm is used for non-titled persons, gold for peers.

The armet This helm, with the visor open or closed and with or without bars, is used in Italian and Spanish Heraldry and, to a lesser extent, in France. Its style is quite different from that of the other helms used in European Heraldry, so that its use in an Achievement may give a good clue to the bearer's origins.

All the European sovereigns have used gold helms, facing the front and topped by a royal crown. In England the royal helm shows eight bars; others show a gold helm with the visor open.

Although the conventions that govern the use of helms are not rules (despite attempts to standardize the use of helms to indicate the rank of the wearer), there are discernible national styles that should help students to discover the origin and rank of the wearer. But the helm alone is never conclusive evidence; it should be considered with caution and assessed in the context of the style of the other items of the Achievement.

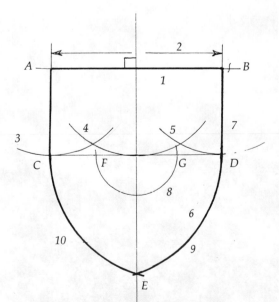

A simple method for constructing a quartered shield: draw two squares hanging from the line AB and from the points F and G respectively make the two arcs DE and CE. The proportions of the shield can be altered by altering the positions of F and G.

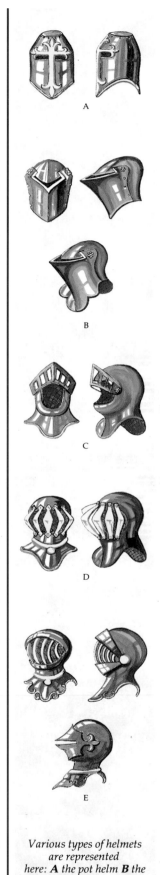

*Various types of helmets are represented here: **A** the pot helm **B** the tilting helm **C** the helm with open visor and no bars **D** the barred helm **E** the armet.*

THE CREST

It will be seen from looking at any Achievement of Arms that shows a helmet that it is very unusual for the helmet to have nothing placed upon it. Usually a helmet bears a crest. The crest is a product of the tournament, and because of the importance of pageantry and display in a tournament, the crest, which was proudly fixed atop the helm, became increasingly complicated and large. Every kind of emblem, carved of wood or made of leather and stiffened canvas and richly painted and gilded, was devised and the devices chosen were representations of every kind of thing imaginable. Sometimes they repeated the devices on the armorial bearings, or a part of them; often they were any other thing, real or imaginary, that could be contrived to sit securely atop the helm.

In England nowadays the practice is for all members of a family to exhibit the same crest, but there are several instances of unrelated families displaying similar crests, so that the crest is not a reliable emblem of identification. When family ties and tradition are felt to be important, the crest is displayed on its own, especially on items such as rings, silver, china and glass, that are likely to be handed down from one generation to the next.

On the Continent, where families display the same armorial bearings, each member sports a different crest, by which he may be recognized. It is therefore a very personal emblem. It was often the practice, before a tournament, for helmets, with their crests, to be displayed for inspection, especially by ladies of the court. If a lady espied the crest of someone who had in any way wronged any of her number, she would touch the helm and it would be thrown to the floor by a Herald. The owner was not then able to take part in the tournament and there was nothing for it but for him to pick up his helm and slink off in disgrace.

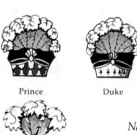

Prince   Duke   Count

Baron

Knight

Napoleonic caps, each with its distinctive headband and plumage to denote rank, were introduced into republican France by the Emperor Napoleon to dissociate French Heraldry from the abolished monarchy.

LEFT A chair-back in the House of Lords, worked in tapestry representing the Royal arms of England; the   *crest is a lion statant (standing), guardant (front-facing), above a Royal crown on a gold helm with seven bars.*

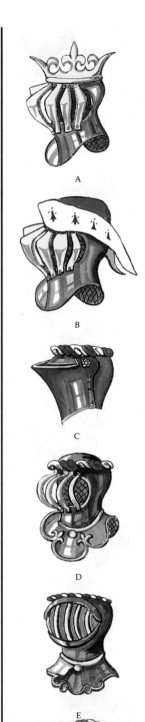

A

B

C

D

E

F

A the crest coronet B the chapeau C, D and E the torse or wreath and F the Spanish torse.

THE TORSE OR WREATH, THE CHAPEAU, THE CREST CORONET

When it became necessary to modify the rules of the tournament, because so many good men were being killed, one of the new customs was to supply each knight with a club, so that — opponents could strike at one another, mounted on their horses, until the crest of one or the other had been knocked to the ground, and the loser mataphorically toppled into the dust! The crest was secured to the top of the helm as securely as possible and the crude fixings were covered by the following three items.

The torse or wreath This is always represented by different coloured materials, twisting together and tied round the helm to cover the gap between the crest and helm. It is thought to have originated from the tournament, when a knight would collect from the crowd a favour from his favourite lady to show that he fought for her honour and as her champion and would tie it round his helm. In Great Britain it now consists of six twists of alternating colour, always with a metal colour (silver or gold) first. On the Continent it is often of five or seven segments, so that a symmetrical design is produced. In Italy a slim torse of ten or twelve sections is used. In Spain, where crests are not used, untitled persons use a plume of ostrich feathers, which are held in place by a torse placed vertically over the crown of the helm. The torse is also used in France, in both forms, and in Holland and Germany.

The chapeau In Great Britain, helms are sometimes seen with the crest standing on what appears to be a red cap with a turned-up ermine lining, which is placed over the top of the helm, with no torse. This is a symbol of royal privilege and is seldom encountered. In Scotland, hereditary barons use a blue chapeau as an emblem of their rank.

The crest coronet Often found atop a helmet is a crest coronet, in place of the torse, out of which issues the crest. This simple coronet is found throughout Europe and the crest coronet should not be confused with a coronet of rank, which is displayed by peers, princes and sovereigns. It has been used as decorative feature, perhaps to invest the wearer with a dignity tht he might otherwise not have. It should be pointed out that Spain and Italy uses coronets of rank with no crest atop the helm, although in Italy the coronet always sits on a narrow torse. Italy, like Spain, does not use crests. Helms with coronets of rank are found in Russian, Polish, Hungarian and Scandinavian Heraldry. Apart from their decorative function, the torse, the wreath and the crest coronet are all designed to hold the mantelling in place on the helm.

Napoleon tried to sweep away all French Heraldry associated with royalty and introduced a new system. In the place of helmets and crests a series of black caps, known as Napoleonic caps, each with different plumes and headbands, was introduced to indicate rank.

MANTELLING OR LAMBREQUIN

When the Crusaders went to free the Holy Land, fitted out with all the weaponry, armour and accoutrements of war of medieval knights, they soon discovered that they were ill equipped to fight in a hot, dusty and arid climate. They rapidly adopted the native practice of wearing a small cloak or cloth fastened to the top of the helm to keep the sun off their backs. That covering became known as the mantelling. It became fashionable for knights to have their mantelling slashed to pieces, to show that they had been in many fierce battles. This custom accounts for the fantastic designs and shapes of mantelling that may be encountered, from the simple, restrained kerchief hanging at the back of the helm (usually seen with a pot helm) to the wildly extravagant swirls and masses that have become so exaggerated that they have earned the description 'mass of seaweed'.

It is usual for the mantelling to be of two colours, the principal metal colour of the armorial bearings on the inside and on the outside the principal colour. In describing mantelling the outside colour is always mentioned first, and then the inside, describing the latter as 'turned or doubled', whichever it may be. It is not unusual to find mantelling of two or more outside colours, nor to find them turned, doubled or lined with a fur, or with metals of different colours. You may find the outside strewn with devices, sometimes echoing those displayed on the shield, or find them covered with badges. Sometimes, when the crest is an animal or person, the mantelling is a continuation of the skin of the animal or the vesture of the person.

THE USE OF MORE THAN ONE HELM AND CREST

When different armorial Achievements become invested in one person, it is quite common to find more than one helm and crest used on an Achievement; in German Heraldry as many as twelve may be used. In Great Britain, where it is unusual to find more than three, it is the practice to place all the helms facing the dexter. On the Continent they are placed to respect each other, the most important on the dexter side, or in the middle if there are more than two.

CORONETS OF RANK

In the Achievements of peers, it is common to find displayed between the shield and the helms the coronet of rank. This is common practice in most European countries, except Spain, Portugal and Italy, where no crest is used and the coronet is placed on the helm. It is also common for peers simply to display a shield showing their armorial devices and their coronets of rank. It is important not to confuse coronets of rank with crest coronets or Heraldic crowns.

INSIGNIA OF OFFICE

It is quite common for insignia denoting some office held by the bearer of the Achievement — such as the two crossed batons of the Earl Marshal of England — to be placed behind the shield.

ANCIENT DESIGN

FANCIFUL ELABORATION

MODERN DESIGN

Three designs of mantelling.

PRINCE

DUKE

MARQUIS

EARL

VISCOUNT

BARON

Each rank of the English nobility has its own coronet, as illustrated here.

RIGHT *The armorial bearings of Sir Ronald Gardner-Thorpe show the circlet of a Knight of the British Empire, with the badge of the order on the ribbons below, and the Cross of the order of the Knights of St John.*

THE CHAINS, MEDALS & CROSSES OF ORDERS OF CHIVALRY

It is not uncommon to find placed behind the shield a cross of an order of chivalry, which denotes that the bearer is a knight commander of the relevant order. Ribands of chivalric orders of knighthood, with the motto of the order on them, are also found encircling shields. Knights of the order may encircle their riband with the chain collar of the order. Badges or decorations, of an order, in the lesser ranks, may be hung below the shield, shown suspended from ribands.

SUPPORTERS

On many Achievements of Arms the shield and the helm sometimes appear as if they were held up by two animals or other beings, acting as supporters. This practice emanates from the earliest Heraldic times and is thought to have been begun by seal engravers, filling in the space between the side of the engraved shield and the round edge of the seal with mythical beasts such as small dragons. The practice of using supporters probably became widespread with the rise of the tournament at which knights employed their pages to parade around the arena, carrying their masters' shields and dressed in fantastic costumes, to the delight of the crowd.

Supporters may take any form, from animals or humans to mythical or celestial beings. It is more usual to find two supporters, one on each side, although frequently only one is used.

The use of supporters varies greatly from country to country and care should be taken not to confuse supporters that are properly part of the Achievement of Arms with those that have been added purely for artistic effect.

In Great Britain, supporters may be granted by the appropriate authority as part of the Achievement of Arms and handed down from father to son. They may be used by peers, knight commanders of the orders of chivalry, civic authorities and corporate bodies. The same is true in Scotland, where their controlled use is also extended to some barons and clan chiefs. In the Netherlands there are no restrictions on their use. In Germany and Austria they are used only by the higher ranks of the peerage; but there is no definite rule and peers quite often do not use them. It is common for the national arms of this area, and those of its sovereigns and princes, to use one supporter, the eagle, in its many forms, with the shield displayed on the breast. Italy, Spain and Portugal generally do not use supporters. In Belgium their use is generally confined to the nobility and to some civic authorities.

Supporters can be two identical beings or two that are completely dissimilar. They may be carrying any kind of weapon or banner or any

*The three Coats of Arms shown here are **A** the arms of Baron Manvers **B** the arms of the Duke of Argyll (showing the emblem of the Hereditary Grand Master of the Household and Hereditary Justice-General of Scotland), and **C** the arms of the Earl Marshal of England (showing the batons of office and the blue ribbon of the Garter).*

SALVUS IN IGNE

RIGHT *An achievement of arms with griffin supporters.*

The Achievement of Arms of the Borough of Beccles
follows the usual practice of including two supporters.

other object appropriate to the bearer. Flying birds are sometimes used, or two ships.

It is perfectly permissible to show armorial bearings that should have supporters without them; for although they may form part of a grant of armorial bearings they are, like everything else but the shield, not essential elements of an Achievements.

THE MANTEAU OR ROBE OF ESTATE AND PAVILION

Princes, the higher representatives of the nobility and certain high officials of secular bodies or the Church display their whole Achievements upon a representation of a draped cloak, usually with a colour outside and one of the furs within. There are many varieties of this custom, though it is not practised in Great Britain.

THE COMPARTMENT

In most instances it is felt that the supporters should have something to stand upon and this is know as the compartment. (though there are plenty of examples of Achievements with supporters left hanging in the air, as is were, without compartments). The compartment may consist of almost anything. It may represent solid ground (often strewn with herbage or flowers, or badges), water or simply ornamental scroll work. A motto riband is sometimes used.

THE MOTTO

Mottoes are found in many Achievements. In Scotland they are regarded as an essential ingredient and are placed on a riband above the helm. In England, as on the Continent, they are not regarded as part of the Achievement, but they may, if desired, be placed below the shield. The riband is usually drawn as ornately as the style and period allow and is usually shown white outside and of a colour on the reverse.

BADGES

It is quite common to find a badge as part of an Achievement. A badge is a simple Heraldic device that belongs to the bearer, but which other people can wear to show their allegiance to him or his cause. A badge would be worn by the retainers, messengers and soldiers of the bearer. In the days when knights held tenure of their lands in exchange for military service, they would come to the battle in their own coat of arms, but also displaying the badge of their overlord. Badges survive today and are worn by military units, fire brigades, police forces, schools and universities and the like.

Badges are sometimes arranged into the composition of an Achievement, so as to be included with it but not form part of it; they may also be found strewn on the compartment or mantelling.

ABOVE Badges of the St John family on the tomb of Nicholas St John; TOP LEFT the sun in splendour, CENTRE a fetlock.

LEFT A stone carving by S & J Winter illustrates the use of a single supporter in Heraldry.

BELOW LEFT The armorial bearings of the Chelmsford Borough Council, engraved by Stefan Oliver, have an unusual compartment, consisting of a bridge over water, retained by a motto riband.

CHAPTER FIVE
Armorial Bearings

THE SHIELD is the one indispensable part of an Achievement. It now bears the armorial bearings of a person, which would otherwise be borne on his Coat of Arms, horse trappings, flags, banners, sail or what you will. It is from the Coat of Arms that we derive the name now used to describe the shield, and what is displayed on it. In modern parlance this has been shortened simply to 'arms'. One applies to the appropriate Heraldic authority for a grant of 'arms' (short for 'armorial bearings'). At the same time the other items to be included in the Achievement, as appropriate to the applicant's rank and circumstances, are assigned. The term, 'Coat of Arms', therefore, has become synonymous with the shield and what is displayed upon it. All modern designs of armorial bearings are prepared with a view to their being displayed upon a shield; and it is therefore important to understand what is displayed, since these symbols and emblems are the mainstay of Heraldry.

THE BLAZON

A written description of a Coat of Arms may at first appear to make little sense; but once you become used to the language and the way that it is set out, you will find that a well-written description is a masterpiece of concision that should enable any artist to draw correctly everything that is displayed on the shield. This description is known as the 'blazon'. To 'blazon' a coat of arms is to describe it in words. To 'emblazon' it, is to paint or draw it in full colour. Because the blazon always follows a set pattern, we will consider what might be painted on a shield in the same order.

BELOW Ancient examples of Coats of Arms bearing a plain tincture only are (from left to right) those of Bruget of Normandy ('argent'), Berrington of Chester ('azure') and the Duke of Brittany ('ermine').

PER PALE

PER SALTIRE

QUARTERLY

GYRONY

MASONY

As the number of gentlemen bearing arms increased, single-tincture Coats of Arms were no longer sufficient, despite the variety of charges placed upon them, to distinguish one from another. Two-coloured shields were therefore introduced. Illustrated here and overleaf are the various methods of dividing a shield.

PER PALE

PER FESSE

PER BEND

PER BEND SINISTER

PER CHEVRON

TIERCED IN PAIRLE

THE FIELD

Before any design is placed on a shield, the shield is painted a colour, which can be one of the metals, colours or furs. There are examples of Coats of Arms that consisted of a plain tincture only. Bruget of Normandy bore a Coat of Arms and a shield 'argent' (silver or white), the Duke of Brittany bore 'ermine' and Berrington of Chester bore 'azure'. Notwithstanding all the things imaginable that might be placed on a blue shield, for example, it was soon necessary for differentiation to use two-coloured shields, with one half red, say, and the other white.

A field semy, semé, strewn or powdered Sometimes a field will be found strewn with many small charges and these are usually of a stated colour. Some of them have their own special terms: 'Semy de lis' or 'semy of fleur de lis' means 'representing the lily', while 'crusiley' means that the field is strewn with little crosses. Other terms are 'of the roundles', 'pomme', 'bezanty', 'platy', 'of the goutees' and 'goutty d'or'.

The divisions of the field The shield can be divided in a variety of ways and the form of the division and the colours to be used are always mentioned first in the blazon. Each different form of division of the field, has its own term, each of which is illustrated below. When describing a divided field, the colour in the top dexter corner is always given first.

The lines of partition In all the examples shown, the divisions are made with straight lines. They can, however, be made with a variety of zigzag or wavy lines, which are shown below. In a blazon the order of description is as follows: the division of the field (if any), the configuration of the line (if not straight) and the colours, the top dexter being first.

THE CHARGES

Any item placed upon the field of the shield is known as a charge. If a shield has anything placed on it, it is said to be charged with that object. Similarly a lion with a rose on its shoulder is described as being 'charged on the shoulder with a rose'.

It has become the custom in an illustration of a Coat of Arms to show any charge placed upon the field as casting a shadow. As well as enhancing the artistic effect, the shadow shows that the item is not part of the field, but is 'charged' upon it. The light is always shown as coming from the dexter top. The provision of a shadow is, however, by no means a rule and in small works it is frequently omitted for the sake of clarity. Charges of all kinds can themselves be charged in never-ending successions and combinations.

The ordinaries This main group of charges consists of geometric shapes placed upon a shield, stripes in different combinations and other shapes. An ordinary usually takes up about one-third of the area of the shield. It is import-

BARRY

BENDY

BENDY SINISTER

PALY

LOZENGY

CHEQUEY

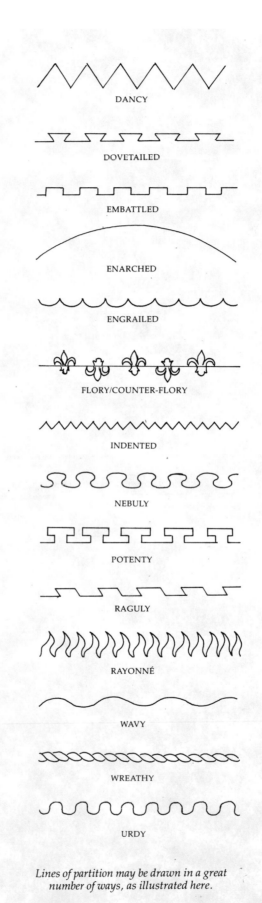

DANCY

DOVETAILED

EMBATTLED

ENARCHED

ENGRAILED

FLORY/COUNTER-FLORY

INDENTED

NEBULY

POTENTY

RAGULY

RAYONNÉ

WAVY

WREATHY

URDY

Lines of partition may be drawn in a great number of ways, as illustrated here.

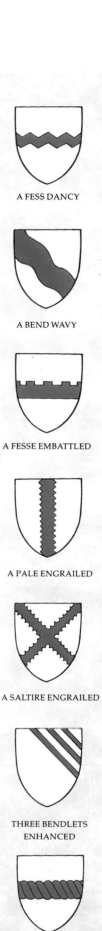

A FESS DANCY

A BEND WAVY

A FESSE EMBATTLED

A PALE ENGRAILED

A SALTIRE ENGRAILED

THREE BENDLETS ENHANCED

A FESSE WREATHY

Various ways in which lines of partition may divide a shield are illustrated here.

LEFT *An achievement of arms of one of the many armigerous Smith families, showing argent on a fess* nebuly counter-nebuly sable three rabbits' heads erased argent, in the second and third quarters.

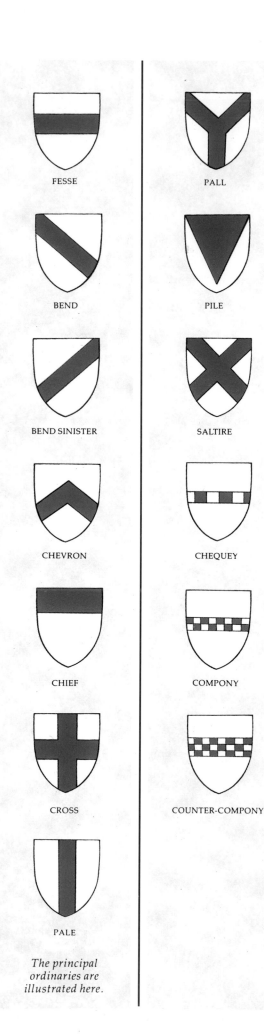

FESSE

PALL

BEND

PILE

BEND SINISTER

SALTIRE

CHEVRON

CHEQUEY

CHIEF

COMPONY

CROSS

COUNTER-COMPONY

PALE

The principal ordinaries are illustrated here.

ant to remember that an ordinary is not a division of the field, but a charge placed upon it. All the main ordinaries are illustrated.

The subordinaries These are smaller geometric charges, less frequently used, but no less important. These too can soon be learned and, once remembered, are easily recognized.

The roundles and gutte The roundles appear as different coloured circles each with their own name. A gold roundle is a bezant, a silver roundle is called a plate, red, a torteau, blood-red, a guze, blue, a hurt, green, a pomme, black, a pellate, ogress or gunstone, purple a golpe, orange, an orange, and when barry, wavy, argent and azure, a fountain.

'Gutte' (or 'gutty', 'goutty') means 'strewn with droplets'. Like the roundles, they have a different name for each colour. Care should be taken not to confuse these with the many forms of ermine spot. 'Gutty d'or' describes a field or charge strewn with gold drops, 'gutty d'eau', silver drops, 'gutty de sang', red drops, 'gutty des larmes', blue drops, 'de poix', black drops, and 'd'huile' (or more rarely, 'd'olive') green drops.

Combinations Combinations of these groups are frequently seen and a few examples are set out below.

Countercharging This very attractive feature is quite often encountered and it presents some impossible-looking combinations of shape and colour until the idea is mastered: a charge is placed over a divided field and the colours are reversed. Some exciting and exotic effects can be produced by this very simple method, some examples of which are shown so that you will recognize it when you see it.

Other charges Any object may be placed upon a shield either on its own or in combination with the ordinaries, subordinaries, or other unrelated objects. Charges may be of any colour, including their own natural colour, and they may be counter-charged with the field or the ordinaries or be themselves charged with other charges. The variety is endless, and needs to be, to ensure that each Coat of Arms is unique. The only limitations are those imposed by good taste and the rule of tincture concerning the use of colour, metal and fur.

Canting arms Mention has several times been made of charges that relate to the name of the bearer. This was a very common practice and is still carried on wherever possible. Unfortunately, with the change of language, the meaning of the allusion has often been lost.

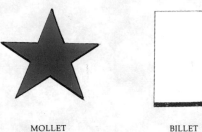

MOLLET

BILLET

TWO BARS

TWO BARS GEMEL

BARRULET

BATON

TWO BENDLET

The sub-ordinaries are illustrated here.

DESCRIBING A SHIELD

There are two ways, apart from painting or drawing a detailed picture of the Coat of Arms, in which it may be described.

The first, (as has already been briefly mentioned), is the blazon. It is quite tricky to master, until you get the hang of it. All blazons follow a set pattern. Firstly they describe the divisions of the field, if there are any, and the partition lines, if they are not straight. They consider next the main charge, then any secondary charges that may be placed either side of the main charge, and next any other charges that may be placed on the main charge. A careful study of the two examples shown here will reveal the technique. Practice with a published armorial (to be found in most libraries) is a good way to develop the knack.

The second is a method known as 'the trick'. This is a shorthand method of annotating a Coat of Arms — the sort of note that might be made to serve as a reminder of a Coat of Arms seen, say, on a public building, in order to identify it later. This is the main use for the abbreviations found in Heraldry and they are very quickly learned.

BORDURE

CANTON

THREE CHEVRONELS

BEND COTISED

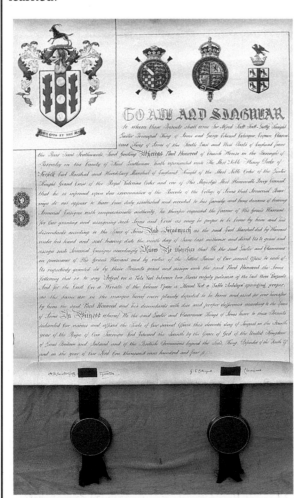

FLANCHES

CROSS FIMBRATED

FRET

FRETTY

GYRON

ESCUTCHEON

ORLE

CROSS QUARTER-PIERCED

TRESSURE

DOUBLE TRESSURE

CROSS VOIDED

ABOVE *The grant of arms of the Henwood family of Kent; such documents conferring arms are issued in the same* form by the Heralds of England and Scotland to the present day.

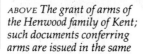

LOZENGE

FUSIL

RUSTRE

MASCLE

ANNULET

Among the ordinaries are included some abstract shapes.

A

B

C

D

Four combinations of ordinaries and subordinaries are illustrated here: **A** *argent a fesse between two chevrons gules (Fitzwalter)* **B** *per pale azure and gules overall a bend or (Langton)* **C** *argent two chevrons with a bordure gules (Albini), and* **D** *argent a saltire and chief gules (Bruce).*

A

B

C

D

Counter-charging may be done in a number of ways. Illustrated here are four examples: **A** *per chevron argent and gules overall a crescent counter-charged (Barker)* **B** *per pale argent and gules overall a bend counter-charged (Chaucer)* **C** *argent a pile and a chevron counter-charged, and* **D** *per pale or and gules a chevron counter-charged (Chambers)*

A

B

C

D

These four illustrations are examples of canting arms: **A** *argent between three calves sable a fesse gules (Calverly)* **B** *argent a squirrel gules eating a gold nut (Squires)* **C** *azure three hedgehogs argent (Harris), and* **D** *argent between three moorcocks a chevron sable (Moore).*

A

B

C

D

A shield has four main elements to be described in a blazon: **A** *the colour of the shield (azure)* **B** *the main charges (on a chevron)* **C** *the secondary charges (between three billets argent), and* **D** *any additional charges (three torteaux).*

BIRDS IN HERALDRY

There are a number of terms that apply to all birds in Heraldry.

ADDORSED With the wings back-to-back.

ARMED Of the colour of the claws.

BEAKED Of the colour of the beak, as in a 'swan argent beaked gules'.

BELLED Of a falcon, with the falconer's bell attached.

CLOSE Standing on the ground with wings closed.

CROWNED With a crown on its head of the specified colour.

DISPLAYED Of a bird placed on the shield affrontly, with both wings and the legs and tail spread out and head turned to the dexter (with two heads, then each looking outwards).

DOUBLE-HEADED With two heads and neck, joined at the shoulders.

ELEVATED With wing tips pointing upwards.

GORGED With a collar encircling the neck or gorge.

INVERTED With the wing tips turned down.

JESSED Of a falcon, with the bell tied on to the leg with a jess.

MEMBERED Of the colour of the legs.

RISING Of the bird standing on the ground with wings raised.

SOARING Flying like an eagle or lark.

VOLANT Flying across the shield.

VULNING Wounding.

EMBOWED

NAIANT

HAURIENT   URIANT

DEMI-LUCE

Illustrated here are the common postures of Heraldic fish.

ESCALLOP

WHELK

The escallop is a more common shell in Heraldry than the whelk

RIGHT *The tomb of Lord Hunsdon in the St John the Baptist Chapel of Westminster Abbey; among his other armorial cognizances is his crest, a swan wings addorsed and elevated proper.*

Crests commonly feature ostrich feathers, as does the famous badge of the Prince of Wales.

ABOVE RIGHT These arms show the use of a woodwose as a supporter on the right; human monsters are usually employed as supporters in this way, rather than as charges. An exception is the shield of the Wood family, which shows three woodwoses in fesse.

The wings of a bird, when back-to-back, are called addorsed.

A bird with all its limbs spread out is called displayed.

Double-headed describes a bird with two heads and necks, joined at the shoulders.

The falcon, usually shown as a peregrine, was a treasured possession of medieval sportsmen.

Rising *describes a bird on the ground with raised wings.*

Shown here is a bird soaring.

OPPOSITE This stained-glass window, made by Jane Gray, shows the arms of the Worshipful Company of Launderers.

Bird limbs are found both erased and couped.

Practically every type of bird has been used in Heraldry at one time or another. There seem to be no examples of birds eggs being used. The following are the birds which are found most frequently.

EAGLE As the lion is the king of the animals, so the eagle is the king of birds, the fiercest, boldest, and noblest of all. It is usually represented displayed in a very stylized form. It is quite often found as a single supporter, carrying the shield upon its chest.

FALCON The falcon was beloved of medieval sportsmen, so much so that the birds lived in the houses with their masters, with perches provided in each room. The falcon is usually depicted as the peregrine, unless of a special type.

SWAN Used as a charge, crest, supporter or badge, the swan is usually shown white and is usually a penn (male swan), unless otherwise blazoned.

PELICAN The pelican is usually shown as a female tearing her breast to give to her young, which is blazoned 'a pelican in her piety'. She was used as an early symbol for Christ.

MARTLET A representation of the swift, the martlet is shown without feet.

OWL This bird is a symbol of learning.

DOVE An ancient symbol representing the Spirit of God and of Peace, the dove is used in the arms of the College of Heralds in London to symbolize the early role which Heralds played as messengers, ambassadors and peacemakers. Pigeons have been used to carry messages since the Egyptian civilization.

FISHES & SHELLS, INSECTS & REPTILES

Practically every known creature has been employed in the services of Heraldry and these last groups are as important as the more impressive beasts of the field.

—— THE FISHES ——

The dolphin must be the commonest of fish, but all kinds are employed, in all the postures so far described for other beings. Fish also have some terms of their own.

EMBOWED Formed in a graceful curve, usually as of a dolphin.

NAIANT Swimming across the shield, heads to the dexter.

HAURIENT Swimming up to the top of the shield.

URIANT Swimming down to the bottom of the shield.

Fish are frequently used in arms to allude to the name of the bearer and they sometimes appear of no specified type. They can be used as charges and crests. The crest of the Solomon Islands, for example, has an alligator and a shark haurient as supporters and that of the Bahamas bears a swordfish and a flamingo.

CLEANLINESS · IS · NEXT · TO · GODLINESS

FAR LEFT *Illustrated here are the armorial bearings of the Worshipful Company of Vintners.*

CENTRE LEFT *The arms of the United States display the eagle as a single supporter.*

NEAR LEFT *The figure of St Margaret is used as a crest for the arms of the Borough of Lowestoft.*

THE SHELLS

The escallop is the most commonly used shellfish, and frequently denotes that the bearer has been on a pilgrimage or is a pilgrim in the metaphorical sense of the word. Three escallop shells on a shield cannot be taken to mean that the bearer has been on three pilgrimages. Whelk shells also appear.

THE INSECTS

The bee as a symbol of industry is popularly used, as is the spider. Other insects only rarely appear.

THE REPTILES

Lizards and snakes appear, but are not very common. Other reptiles are rare, though there are modern examples of crocodiles.

NOWED Knotted, as applying, for example, to a snake or lizard tail.

COILED With the head erect and in a posture ready to strike.

GLISSANT Gliding.

HUMAN AND CELESTIAL BEINGS

Human and celestial beings occur frequently in Heraldry and all the appropriate terms applied to beasts and birds apply to them as well.

CELESTIAL BEINGS

It is more common to find allusion to heavenly people by symbol than by direct representation. Examples do exist of Christ on the Cross, but very rarely, since it was felt to be improper to reduce so sacred a subject to Heraldry. Though Inverness in Scotland bears 'gules upon a cross the figure of Our Lord crucified proper', most of the very few representations of Christ, of his mother or of the saints are found on the arms of ecclesiastical establishments. Some European towns display saints, but this is not a common practice. Angels occasionally appear as supporters, both officially and unofficially, but again the practice is rare. In modern Heraldry an angel is usually represented as a female figure, vested in a long robe, with wings. Historically angels belonged to a variety of different orders, each portrayed differently. Angel supporters are frequently used to display shields, as a decorative feature, when shown in churches.

THE ARCHANGELS Archangels were definitely felt to be gentlemen in the medieval imagination and arms were attributed to them. The only one of heraldic significance is St. Michael. He is usually depicted in armour, carrying out the fight against the Devil, who is represented by a green dragon. His arms were a red cross on a white field. He was evidently the model for the mythical St. George, who is now the patron saint of chivalry and of England.

CHERUB He is shown as the face of a boy, above a pair of wings.

SERAPHIM He is shown as a man's face, with six wings, but only rarely.

HUMAN BEINGS

The whole human figure is often used as a supporter in all kinds of costume and styles, but it is comparatively rare to find it as a charge, for which purpose it is more common to find hands, heads, legs and hearts, either vested or armoured, in a large variety of ways.

WOODWOSE These are wild men and women of the woods, usually depicted as hairy all over and wearing a few leaves around the loins. Parts of the human body can be erased or couped in the same way as parts of animal bodies.

HEAD — *profile* the head is placed facing dexter. It can be cut off at the neck or across the shoulders and the type — a maiden, a Saxon, a Saracen, a Turk and so on — should be specified in the blazon. It can wear any kind of crown or wreath.

DEMI-FIGURE This is a very common crest, and may be armoured (in armour), habited (vested) or vested (dressed in). It is often carrying an object and is sometimes seen wearing a helm and the crest itself repeated in little.

ARMS are often found as charges and crests. As crests they are usually found holding something in the hand. The blazon will sometimes say which arm it is. A 'cubit arm' is one arm cut off cleanly below the elbow. 'Embowed' means 'bent at the shoulder', 'Vambraced' means 'in armour' and 'Vested and cuffed' means 'within a sleeve with a different coloured cuff'.

HANDS Hands are commonly used as a charge. The blazon will always say if right or left. 'Apaumy' means 'open, showing the palm' and 'Closed' means 'clenched or grasping an object'.

LEGS Legs are found used in the same way. Whether they are cut off at, above or below the knee will be stated in the blazon. Arms and legs can be placed either vertically ('palewise') erect or horizontally ('fesswise').

LEFT The armorial bearings of Sir Edmund Bedingfeld were engraved on a glass pitcher by Stefan Oliver.

ABOVE An illustration from Froizart's Chronicles, a 14th century manuscript; the English army campaign in France under the banner of St George.

OPPOSITE FAR RIGHT Church funeral hatchments; the hatchment on the right shows 'or three piles piercing a human heart gules' for Hart Logan.

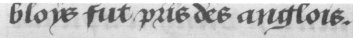

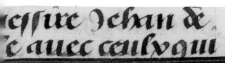

FAR LEFT *The arm is described as 'vambraced' (in armour), holding a battle-axe.*

LEFT *This illustration shows a cubit arm (cut off cleanly below the elbow); it is described as vested because of the sleeve; vested and cuffed, in a blazon, means that the cuff is of a different colour from the sleeve.*

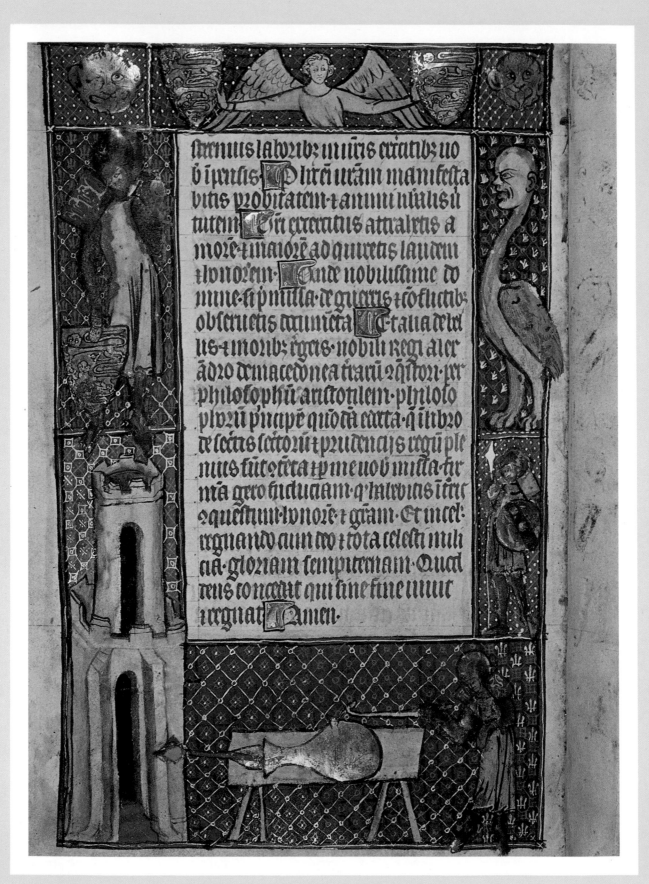

An illuminated canon (1326) from Christchurch,
Oxford, showing an angel bearing the Royal arms of
England.

CHAPTER SIX
The Animal Kingdom

*O*F ALL the charges used in Heraldry animals and monsters stick most in people's minds. They are extensively used on shields, crests and badges as well as serving as supporters. Beasts always face the dexter when used as a charge, crest or badge, unless otherwise stated, and they always look where they are going, that is to the dexter, again unless otherwise stated. The tail is usually shown erect and curved, in a style according to custom or the discretion of the artist, unless otherwise stated.

There are a number of terms that apply to all animals and monsters collectively classified as beasts.

ARMED When applied to beasts, the term 'armed' refers to beaks, claws, tusks, horns and the like. The term usually occurs when these are of a different colour from the beast itself, as in 'a lion rampant sable, armed gules'.

AFFRONTY Facing the front.

BICORPORATE OR TRICORPORATE One head with two or three bodies.

CRINED With a mane or head of hair, separately tinctured.

COWED With the tail down between the legs.

DEMI The top half of the body only, usually with tail included.

DISARMED With no beak, claws, horns or tusks.

DOUBLE-QUEUED With two tails.

GUARDANT Looking at the observer, full-faced, directly out of the shield.

GORGED With the neck or gorge encircled (by a coronet, for example).

HORNED OR TUSKED In *armed*, above.

LANGUED With a tongue of a specified colour.

NOWED Tied in a knot, usually of the tail.

QUEUE FOURCHY OR FOURCHÉE With a forked tail.

REGARDANT looking backwards.

SINISTER Facing the other way, to the sinister, as in 'a lion rampant sinister'.

TUFTED With tufts of hair.

UNGULED Of the hoofs of an animal, when their colour is different from the colour of the body, as in 'unicorn argent, unguled or'.

VULNED Wounded and bleeding.

A lion guardant *has its face towards the viewer.*

A lion double-queued *has two tails.*

A forked tail is called a queue fourchy.

A lion looking backwards *is called* regardant.

TOP *A* lion demi *is drawn with the top half of the body only, but usually including the tail.*

ABOVE *A lion* couchant *is drawn lying down in an alert posture.*

ABOVE *The tomb of Richard Berghersh in Lincoln Cathedral; the first and second shields show a lion queue fourchée (with a forked tail). The shield of the Suffolk branch of the family was argent (white), a chief gules (with a red top section covering one third of the shield), overall a lion rampant queue fourchée or.*

An animal facing the front and cut off cleanly below the ears is described as caboshed.

Each of the animals on this badge is described as face, *meaning with a head caboshed.*

An animal facing the side and cut off cleanly behind the ears is described as couped close.

Couped *is the term for an animal cut off at the neck.*

Erased *describes an animal with jagged skin.*

PARTS OF THE BODY

The head and limbs are frequently found as crests, charges and badges and these have special descriptions.

CABOSHED Facing the front and cut off cleanly behind the ears.

COUPED CLOSE Facing the side and cut off cleanly behind the ears.

COUPED Cut off close at the neck.

ERASED As if pulled off, with jagged skin.

FACE A head caboshed.

JESSANT DE LIS A face with a fleur-de-lis behind and thrust out through the mouth.

LIMBS Paws, arms, legs and tails are shown couped (cut off close to the body), or erased.

This illustration shows a face jessant de lis, *with a fleur-de-lis behind, coming through the mouth.*

The limb on the left is couped; *the one on the right is* erased.

Two lions walking in opposite directions are said to be counter passant.

Two lions leaping in opposite directions are said to be counter salient.

A lion at rest is dormant.

Small lions charged on a shield are called lioncells.

THE ANIMALS

Of all the animals the lion is the king. Favoured for his nobility and fierceness, the lion has been used in Heraldry all over the world. He is always displayed looking as fierce and as haughty as the artist can contrive, with his claws extended. His claws and tongue are always painted red, regardless of what colour he is, unless he is on a red field, when they are painted blue. The lion is always shown in one of a variety of set postures, which also apply to other animals. There are a number of terms to describe these postures.

COUCHANT Lying down in an alert posture.

COUNTER PASSANT Two lions walking in opposite directions.

COUNTER SALIENT Two lions leaping in opposite directions.

DORMANT Lying down at rest.

LIONCELLS Small lions, usually in large numbers on a shield.

PASSANT Walking across the shield. A lion 'passant guardant' is known as a leopard; a leopard of England is a 'lion passant guardant or'.

RAMPANT Rearing up in fight.

SALIENT Taking a leap across the shield.

SEJANT Sitting on his haunches. When he sits facing the front he is termed 'affronty'.

STATANT Just standing there.

TWO LIONS ADDORSED Two lions rampant, back to back.

TWO LIONS RESPECTANT OR COMBATANT Two lions rampant, face to face.

Lions are frequently found as supporters in which case they stand holding the shield and, sometimes, the helm as well.

It is common to find the head, arm or paw used as a charge.

It is also common to find lions with collars and chains or with crowns, or carrying something in their paws, or charged on the shoulder with some device. Sometimes they are powdered all over with small charges. There are numerous lion monsters and of these the winged lion and the sea lion are the most common. A lion with a human face and human body and head is also found.

Most animals are found in Heraldry and since the opening up of the New World all kinds of species unknown to earlier Heraldry have been introduced. All of them may appear as supporters, charges or on crests. Some of the most ancient and most common are worth noting.

BEAR He is usually shown standing upright on his back legs, holding a tree trunk, and often with a muzzle (derived, no doubt, from the performing bears at medieval fairs and emblematic of having tamed the savage beast).

BEAVER He is occasionally found, usually as a symbol of industry.

BOAR In medieval times the wild boar was common throughout Europe and regularly hunted. He is a ferocious animal when roused and many people have been killed by his ripping tusks. He

A lion walking across a shield is passant; *when it is also looking at the observer (passant guardant) it is known as a leopard.*

A lion rearing up is rampant.

Salient *describes an animal leaping across a shield.*

A lion on its haunches is sejant.

A lion simply standing, motionless, is described as statant.

Two lions rampant, *back-to-back, are called* addorsed.

Two breeds of hound – the greyhound and the talbot – are traditionally used in Heraldry.

is always shown with powerful tusks and a crest of bristling hair down his back, usually of a different colour. He is usually shown trotting, unless he is a supporter, when he stands on his back legs. He has often been used as a badge. A white boar was the badge of Richard III of England.

BROCK OR BADGER He is occasionally found in all roles. He has also been called a 'grey' and is used as a charge by the de Grise family.

BUCK (FALLOW DEER) He is distinguished from the stag by his wide, bladed antlers.

BULL He is frequently encountered, though usually only the head, with a ring in the nose, is shown. Continental Heraldry makes frequent use of the long, curved horns of the wild bull or auroch, especially on crests, in pairs with pendant feathers.

DEER Species of deer and antelope from the New World are gradually being introduced. Deer have a terminology of their own: when *passant* they are called 'trippant'; when *statant guardant*, described as 'at gaze'; when *couchant*, 'lodged'; when running, 'in chase' or 'at speed'; and when *salient*, 'springing'. Antlers (horns) have their own terms as well; they are called 'attires', and the points 'tines'.

ERMINE A white stoat usually shown as a fur, he is sometimes found as an animal in his own right.

FOX The epitome of slyness and cunning, he is occasionally found.

FROG The emblem of the devil, he is still today associated with witchcraft.

GOAT He is always shown in typical billy-goat form, with a rough coat, curved horns and beard. Specific types of goat are also used.

HEDGEHOG Also called an urchin and, in French, an 'herrison', he is borne by the family of Harris.

HORSE A symbol of speed and bravery, the horse was the emblem of the Saxon kings of England.

He is rarely found, though the head appears as a crest and a charge. He is far more common, of course, in the form of the unicorn.

HOUND Though modern breeds of dog are being introduced into Heraldry, traditionally only two breeds were used: the greyhound, as an emblem for a swift messenger, and the talbot, an ancient hunting dog somewhere between a hound and a Great Dane, as an emblem of faithfulness.

LAMB He is frequently used as an emblem of Christ.

RABBIT He is also known as a 'coney'.

RAM He is sometimes found on arms, though not commonly.

SQUIRREL He is usually shown red in colour, siting on his haunches with a nut.

STAG He is shown as the red deer and is also called hart or royal when of a mature age with twelve points or more on the antlers.

TIGER Modern usage shows the striped animal, as we know it, but in ancient times the tyger (as he is spelled in Heraldry) was so far removed from reality as to warrant being included among the monsters.

WOLF Though common throughout Europe in medieval times, he is not often found.

ABOVE LEFT Shields on a tomb in Lincoln Cathedral (c. 1340); the arms of Bohun (LEFT) are azure between six lioncells or a bend argent cotised or. The shield on the right is Hastings quartering de valence.

BELOW LEFT The arms of the Bishop Goldwell Chantry in Norwich Cathedral; argent a chief or overall a lion rampant ermine.

ABOVE LEFT The ferocious boar is frequently seen on badges.

MIDDLE LEFT The badger, or brock, is sometimes called a 'grey'.

BELOW LEFT The wolf is a rare device in modern Heraldry.

ABOVE LEFT The long, curved horns of the wild bull frequently surmount crests.

ABOVE Heraldic bears often wear a muzzle, derived from their use as performing animals at medieval fairs.

——— THE MONSTERS ———

Monsters in Heraldry are the product partly of mythology and legend, partly of fertile imaginations and partly of ignorance. Heraldic artists composed designs of creatures that they had never seen, based on the tales of travellers who repeated stories heard in far-off lands. However the monsters were created, they offered medieval Heralds perhaps the most colourful devices for Heraldic expression. In the days when the drama and pageant of the tournament and its attendant fairs and entertainments provided the main excitement of the age, the opportunity for display which monsters gave the Heralds was eagerly seized. Someone trying to devise a costume to be worn by his pages as they paraded his shield around the arena had a vast field to exploit once the idea of Heraldic monsters took hold. Think of the costume possibilities for someone trying to express the idea that he was as fierce as a lion, strong as an ox, swift as a horse and cunning as a fox!

The monsters, which, with a few differences, all follow the rules and customs of the animals, fall into several different groups.

WINGED ANIMALS These are ordinary animals given wings to lend them a greater mythological significance, like the winged lion of St. Mark, the winged horse, Pegasus, and so on.

SEA ANIMALS Many animals, especially the lion and the horse, are turned into sea monsters by giving them fish tails or fins. The sea-dog, for example, has fins instead of feet, a fin along the back and a tail like the beaver's.

MYTHOLOGICAL MONSTERS There are numerous mythological monsters, but most of them are variants of the five which follow.

DRAGON He is a four-legged monster with thick, scaly skin like armour, a long tail ending with a sting, bat-like wings and a horned head with a forked tongue, prominent teeth and claws. He can be of any colour.

PHOENIX He is an eagle, with a tuft on his head, rising from the flames.

SALAMANDER He is a lizard, sitting in flames, unhurt.

UNICORN A horse with a long single horn on its head, the unicorn is an animal of great beauty and allure, said to have been used as a symbol for Christ because by legend he could be caught only by a virgin who tamed him.

WYVERN He is in effect a two-legged dragon. When blazoned properly he is green with a red chest and belly and red underwings.

ABOVE LEFT AND ABOVE The addition of fish tails and fins turns land animals into Heraldic sea monsters.

LEFT The dragon can be of any colour; this is the red dragon of Wales.

County of Avon

LEFT A brass plate etched by P G Marden shows sea stags used as supporters by Avon County on its Coat of Arms.

ABOVE The Achievement of Arms of Cynon Valley Borough shown here was moulded in resin.

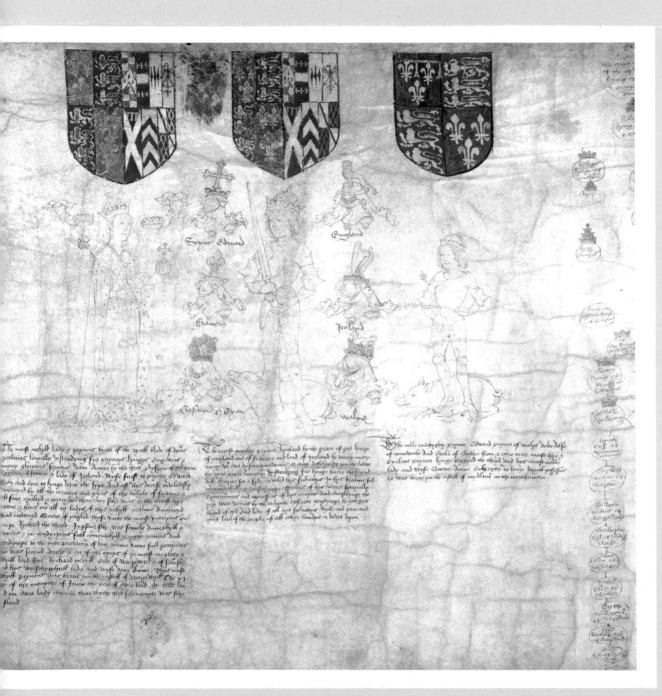

A detail from the Rous Roll, depicting the arms of
Richard III of England and his wife Anne Neville,
showing the boar badge used by him and by his son.

*The chained porcupine crest of the Countess of Sussex,
on her tomb in Westminster Abbey.*

MONSTERS COMPOSED OF MORE THAN ONE ANIMAL

BONICON A bull/horse with curled horns, he is useless for attack, but breaks wind with such effect as to devastate several acres behind him.

COCKATRICE OR BASILISK He is a wyvern with a cockerel's head.

ENFIELD He has a fox's head, a wolf's body, tail and backlegs and an eagle's front legs.

GRIFFIN OR GRYPHON He has the head, breast, wings and foreclaws of an eagle and the body, tail and hind legs of a lion. He also has pointed ear tufts. The griffin is a very strong monster and should always be drawn as such, combining the characteristics of the eagle, king of the birds, with those of the lion, king of the beasts. A griffin *rampant* is said to be 'segreant'. Male griffins have a bunch of long spikes instead of wings and spikes sticking out of other parts of the body.

HERALDIC ANTELOPE He has a lion's body and tail, a dragon's head with long serrated horns, and the legs and hooves of a deer.

HERALDIC TYGER He resembles a lion in form, but with a longer snout, turned-down horn on the end, and tusks in the lower jaw. He is usually coloured bright red. He is very swift and the only thing to do if you wish to steal his cubs is to throw down a mirror, thereby delaying the tyger long enough for you to get away. For this reason he is often shown looking back into a hand mirror on the ground.

OPINICUS He is the same as a griffin, but with four lion's legs.

OUNCE This is a mythical beast resembling the leopard. In Heraldry he is sometimes shown as a black panther.

PANTHER He resembles the real animal in form, but is usually coloured white and covered with multi-coloured spots. He is always shown as in-censed, that is, with flames issuing from his ears and mouth. Some people argue that these are in fact the sweet breath which excites other animals, but puts the fear of death into dragons, on whom the panther preys.

YALE He has the body and legs of a goat, a long nose and tusks like those of a boar. He has two curving horns, which swivel in any direction to fend off attack. One horn is usually shown with pointing forward, the other backwards.

MONSTERS COMPOSED OF HUMAN BEINGS

CENTAUR He has the body and legs of a horse joined to the torso of a man.

HARPY This is usually shown as an eagle with a woman's head and breasts, though sometimes with only the head. Some versions have a woman's torso and head with an eagle's wings and legs.

MANDRAKE This is the head of a man with a poisonous root attached to it.

MELUSIN This is a mermaid with two tails.

MERMAID This is the top half a nude woman and the bottom half a fish tail. She is usually shown looking into a mirror, combing her hair.

MERMAN This is a male mermaid.

SAGITTARY He has the body and limbs of a lion joined to the torso, arms and head of a man.

SPHINX This is not a very common charge in Heraldry. It takes two forms: the Greek sphinx is shown winged with the face and bust of a woman and the body of a lion; the Egyptian sphinx has the face of a man in the head-dress of Pharoah and the body of a lion and is always shown couchant.

TRITON This is a merman holding a trident and blowing into a shell trumpet. He is occasionally shown in armour, as on the arms of the Worshipful Company of Fishmongers in London.

The griffin is always drawn as a powerful, fierce monster; a griffin rampant, *as drawn here, is described as* segreant.

The centaur has the torso of a man and the body and legs of a horse.

The yale has a goat's body and legs, and two horns, one usually shown facing backwards, the other forwards, as here.

FAR LEFT *The lamb is frequently used as a symbol of Christ.*

LEFT *The ounce, a mythical beast resembling a leopard, appears in Heraldry often as a black panther, as here.*

ATTINGO RURA

CHAPTER SEVEN
Plants and Inanimate Objects

ᒪɪᴋᴇ the beasts and birds, all kinds of plants, flowers, leaves and trees appear in general use.

——— THE FLOWERS ———

LILY The queen of the plants is depicted either as the stylized fleur de lis, which can be in a variety of different forms, or as the natural flower.

ROSE The rose, if you like, is the king of the flowers. It is nearly always shown in a stylized form, the Heraldic rose. 'Slipped and leaved proper', which applies to other flowers as well as the rose, means that the outer green sepals and the leaves are shown on a short length of green stalk. 'Seeded' refers to the colours of the centre.

THISTLE This is usually shown 'slipped and leaved proper' as the national emblem of Scotland. It is very much associated with that country and people who have emigrated from it.

QUATREFOIL This is a stylized four-petal flower.

CINQUEFOIL This is a stylized five-petal flower.

These last two are sometimes found with the centre pierced with a hole.

FRAISE (OR FRASE, FRAZE) This is a white cinquefoil representing the strawberry flower and is used on the Coat of Arms of Fraiser, 'gules three fraises'.

——— THE PLANTS ———

BROOM OR PLANTA GENESTA This is a sprig showing the leaves, flowers and pods and is a well-known badge of the Plantagenet kings of England.

TREFOIL LEAF This is a well known three-leafleted charge.

MAPLE LEAF This appears in Canadian Heraldry. The maple leaf is the official emblem of Canada.

HOLLY LEAF This appears in Scottish Heraldry as a charge and is held up in a hand in a crest.

OAK LEAVES These appear throughout Europe, as do acorns.

WHEATEARS These are also quite common throughout most of Europe.

GARB This commonly is a sheaf of wheat, but can be of other things.

——— THE TREES ———

Trees of all kinds appear as charges and crests. They are quite often shown growing 'from a mound'. 'Acorned' means of an oak with acorns. 'Fructed' means with fruit as in the Orange Free State in South Africa, and which bears 'or on a mound vert an orange tree fructed proper'. 'Eradicated' means a tree shown uprooted.

Many stylized versions of the lily are found in Heraldry.

RIGHT Two shields in the stone of Lincoln Cathedral; The Farr shield (LEFT) shows a saltar with four fleur de lis. The shield of Weller (RIGHT) displays three roses.

OPPOSITE LEFT The armorial bearings of the Hambledon District Council were moulded in resin by de Havilland & Howell.

OPPOSITE FAR RIGHT The arms of Astley of Norfolk on Norwich Cathedral, showing a cinquefoil ermine pierced in the first quarter.

The Heraldic rose is nearly always shown in a stylized form. The Tudor Rose of England (right) amalgamates the white rose of the House of Lancaster and the red rose of the House of York.

UNITED IN PROGRESS

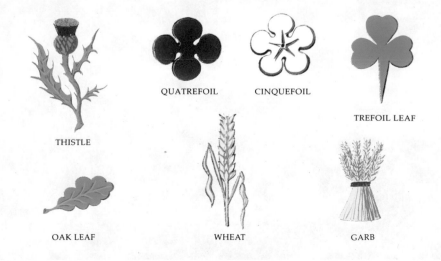

THISTLE

QUATREFOIL

CINQUEFOIL

TREFOIL LEAF

OAK LEAF

WHEAT

GARB

INANIMATE BODIES

This group encompasses all kinds of artefacts, weapons, tools, buildings, ships, every kind of thing imaginable. It is beyond the scope of this book to list everything that might be encountered. The groups are mentioned and attention is drawn to any obscurity or peculiarity in the terms used.

THE CROSS By far the most important item is the cross. Because it is the symbol of Christianity and every Christian state took it as its emblem when it set out on the Crusades, there is a bewildering variety of crosses. Some authorities list more than 150. Most of these are very rare; a dozen of the most common varieties are illustrated.

THE CELESTIAL BODIES

SUN This is usually shown as the 'sun in splendour', sometimes with a face, sometimes not. 'Sun burst' refers to the representation of a ray of sunlight from behind a cloud.

MOON This is shown as a crescent. 'Increscent' refers to a crescent moon facing the dexter; 'Decrescent' refers to a crescent moon facing the sinister; 'In her compliment' refers to the full moon shown with a face to avoid confusion with a plate.

STARS A star is always called an estoile and is shown with six or more wavy rays.

RAINBOW This appears in the Crest of the Hope family.

THUNDERBOLT This appears as a charge, a symbol of wrath, and recently, of electric power.

CLOUDS These are usually seen with something issuing from them, sunrays or a hand.

THE BUILDINGS A wide range of these are used, but except for the three shown — the tower, the castle, and the bridge — most are rare. These appear as charges, crests and badges. (The portcullis, a defensive gate, is also frequently seen).

CRESCENT MOON

INCRESCENT MOON

DECRESCENT MOON

ESTOILE

SUN BURST

MOON IN HER PLENITUDE

TOWER

TOWER TRIPLE-TOWERED

CASTLE

BRIDGE

BRIDGE TRIPLE-ARCHED

PORTCULLIS

WINDMILL SAILS

Illustrated here are the most commonly found buildings in Heraldry.

SILENTIUM STULTORUM VIRTUS

Professor Sir PETER TIZARD MA BM FRCP
MASTER 1983-1984

THE WEAPONS Weapons of all kinds are commonly used throughout Europe and appear as charges, crests and badges and held or brandished by crests and supporters. The most common are the sword, the seax, the battle-axe, the arrow, the arrowhead, the peon, the caltrap, the spear, the tilting spear, the mace and the coronel. The peon is a kind of broad arrowhead and the caltrap is a spiked object which was strewn on the ground to stop horses. The coronel was used to blunt the tip of a tilting spear.

THE SHIPS All kinds of ships have been used in Heraldry and the type is usually specified. 'Lymphand', is a galley (trading vessel) in full sail. (Anchors, fish traps, nets, fish spears and tridents have also been used.)

THE CLOTHING All kinds of clothing — footwear, hats, armour and gloves — are used as charges. Pilgrim staffs and bags are also seen. A 'Maunch' is a sleeve with pocket pendant.

THE DOMESTIC ITEMS Among the most commonly seen domestic items are cups, globes, chess rooks, books, buckles, keys, locks and fetterlocks, mill rinds, clarions, and bougets.

MILL-RIND This is the metal bracket which takes the spindle in the centre of a millstone and holds a tie rod on the outside wall of a building.

CLARION This is a musical instrument, a kind of trumpet.

BOUGET This is a water carrier, consisting of two water buckets made of skin on a yoke.

FLEAN This is a kind of surgical instrument, now obsolete.

THE HERALDIC CROWNS A variety of crowns are used as charges. They have nothing to do with rank, but serve to denote excellence in a sphere of activity. Note that these are termed crowns, not coronets.

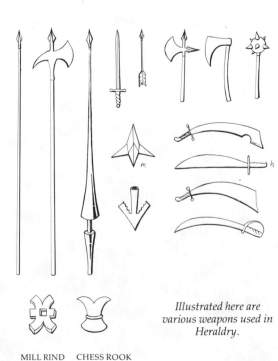

*Ships used in Heraldry include **A** the lymphand **B** the trading vessel, and **C** the Viking ship. Anchors **D** also occur as motifs.*

MILL RIND   CHESS ROOK

Illustrated here are various weapons used in Heraldry.

ASTRAL

ANCIENT

CREST CORONETS

EASTERN

PALISADO

MURAL

SAXON

NAVAL

VALLARY

Many different forms of crowns are used as charges.

CHAPTER EIGHT

Additions to Arms and Marshalling Arms

IN ORDER to distinguish father from son, when both were wearing the same hereditary arms, systems were developed of adding small distinguishing charges to the shield that could be removed or altered as circumstances in the family changed. Except in Scottish Heraldry, those systems have largely dropped out of use. Scotland has developed a system of adding differently tinted borders that have to be registered for each member of the family.

Some brothers changed the tinctures on their arms or altered the charges to show that, though related to the original arms, they were in fact different; but this practice, too, has largely fallen into disuse.

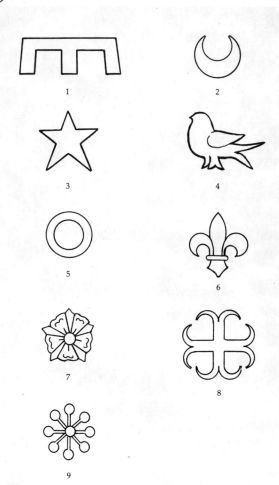

—— AUGMENTATION ——

Throughout Europe it has been the practice of monarchs to reward their subjects for valorous and noble deeds by granting to them some permanent addition to their Coat of Arms. These take many forms, but they are usually a charged canton, chief or escutcheon or even the impalement of a complete Coat of Arms.

MARSHALLING ARMS

It is common to find more than one Coat of Arms displayed on a shield and it is important to understand how this occurs.

—— IMPALEMENT ——

This term refers to two Coats of Arms placed side by side on the same shield. This can happen following a marriage, when the husband's arms appear on the dexter and the wife's on the sinister side of the shield. A person can also impale his arms with the arms of any civic body of which he is the leader, during his tenure of office. The person's arms appear on the sinister and the civic arms on the dexter side of the shield.

—— DIMIDIATION ——

There was a time when only half of each Coat of Arms was placed on the shield. In some cases this practice produced Achievements that were totally unreadable, and it was soon dropped, though some examples still exist that are used today.

—— QUARTERING ——

Quartering means dividing the shield into sections, at least four and sometimes as many as

Augmentation of the coat 'azure issuant from the sinister side a hand and in base a broken fetlock argent' to be permanently impaled by the Barons de Hoeshpied with their own coat of 'argent between 3 crescents sable a chevron gules'.

Augmentation of the addition of a chief of the colours of Belgium to the de Walters family.

An English augmentation of a 'Canton gules a lion passant or' to the coat of More – 'ermine three greyhounds courant sable collared gules'.

twenty-four. In each section a Coat of Arms is placed that has become permanently joined to the original Coat, usually by marriage to an heiress. From the Heraldic point of view, an heiress is the daughter of an armiger who has no sons. If there is more than one daughter, they are heiresses jointly and equally. Because there are no sons to carry the arms into the next generation, an heiress who marries an armiger can hand on her arms to her children as a quartering with their father's Coat. If her husband is not an armiger she cannot pass on her arms. If she is already the heiress to a quartered Coat she can pass on all or a selection of those quarterings, so long as the quartering that brought them into the family is shown. An even number of quarters is usually shown, repeating the paternal Coat in the last quarter if necessary.

Sovereigns also add quarterings to their shields, to demonstrate their sovereignty over different subject states. The Achievement of Arms on the front cover is a good example of this.

------ ESCUTCHEON OF PRETENCE ------

When an armiger marries an Heraldic heiress he places her arms, after her father's death, on a small escutcheon in the middle of his shield. When he dies his sons can display their father's Coat of Arms, quartered with their mother. After a few generations of marriages to heiresses, or to those who subsequently become heiresses because their brothers die, a large number of quarterings can be accumulated. It is important, though often difficult, to distinguish between two quartered Coats impaled on the same shield and one multi-quartered Coat.

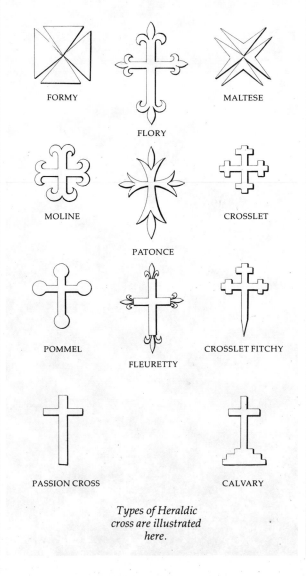

Types of Heraldic cross are illustrated here.

TWO SHIELDS MARSHALLED TOGETHER IN THE SAME ACHIEVEMENT

Occasionally two or more Coats of Arms will be found marshalled together in one Achievement of Arms.

This usually takes place when some honour that is normally indicated by Heraldic accessories placed with the shield, pertains only to one coat and not the other. These circumstances usually occur when a husband who would otherwise impale the arms of his wife with his own wishes to display impaled civic arms to which he is entitled by virtue of some office, order or riband. In these cases he shows his own arms with the required additions beside a shield or lozenge of the arms of his wife. Sometimes, if he has a circlet of an order around his shield, he will place a wreath of flowers or leaves around the arms of his wife to make the Achievement symmetrical. This custom also prevails when a peeress in her own right marries a commoner. The Achievement of the husband is then arranged with the Achievement of the wife. It has become a practice in these circumstances for the helm and the crest to be turned to respect the arms of the wife.

FLAGS

Many different flags are used in Heraldry, their main purpose being to display the Heraldic bearings of their owners, to advertise their presence or to serve as a rallying-point for men in battle.

BANNERS

Historically banners are square and display the bearer's arms upon them, as they would be seen on his coat, armour and shield. Fine examples of these can be seen in St. George's Chapel, Windsor, and Westminster Abbey, where the banners of the present Knights of the Garter and Knights of the Bath, respectively, hang. Any armigerous person can have a banner and fly it from his house when he is present. Banners can also be rectangular, both vertically and horizontally, though in modern parlance the latter shape is generally called a flag. Nowadays most national banner are flag-shaped, like the English Royal Banner, which is universally but quite wrongly called the Royal Standard.

Banners were also used at sea with long streamers of the livery colours. It has been known for arms to be emblazoned on the sails of ships. The Admiral of England in 1436 was the Earl of Huntingdon, who bore on his mainsail the motto, 'England within a bordure of France'. (A bordure is a narrow band running along the edge of a shield.)

PENNONS

The pennon was a small triangular flag carried at the tip of a spear by a knight, showing his personal device. It was made so that the arms were displayed the right way when he was charging and the spear was level.

The banners of the present Knights of the Garter, in St George's Chapel, Windsor.

LIVERY COLOURS

It was the custom of those persons who had retainers to dress them in a uniform so that they could be easily recognized. These uniforms were usually of two colours, usually, though not universally, the chief colour and metal of the bearer's arms. The Tudor kings of England had green and white as their livery colours.

STANDARDS

A standard is a long narrow flag; the longer the flag, the higher the rank of the bearer. It is simply a device for display and pageant, used to present the devices and the livery colour of the bearer.

Though the items displayed on standards have varied in the past, nowadays standards show the arms of the bearer next to the pole. The rest of the standard is divided horizontally into the two livery colours. On this is shown the crest, perhaps repeated, the motto on a riband placed diagonally in as many pieces as are needed and any badge that may be granted. Standards, like badges, are granted by the relevant Heraldic authority to any armigerous person.

MILITARY COLOURS

Military units of all kinds have traditionally carried into battle a banner displaying their badge, their sovereign allegiance and details of their history and battles. Military colours have always been treated with great respect representing as they do the glories and traditions of the regiment. For this reason the colours have been defended with unsurpassed valour in numerous battles. These colours are still proudly displayed today.

HATCHMENTS

It is quite important to mention hatchments, as they are frequently found in churches, often without any explanation of their meaning.

It used to be the custom to paint the Coat of Arms of an armiger on a board and hang it up outside his house when he died. This painting would then be carried to the church at the funeral and afterwards hung there for all time. In the days before newspapers this was the most practical way of letting everyone know that someone had died. The Achievement was always placed on a diamond board and the style of the compsosition indicated which member of the household had died. The clue, apart from the Heraldic accoutrements, lay in the background of the board, which was painted black behind the arms of the deceased.

RIGHT The banner of the present Knights of the Bath in the Henry VII chapel, Westminster Abbey.

ABOVE FAR RIGHT The Turberville window in Bere Regis Church in Dorset; the Turberville arms are impaled with their many spouses.

BELOW FAR RIGHT The arms of Sir William Clopton (1591–1618) impaling those of his first wife, Anne, daughter of Sir Thomas Barnadiston.

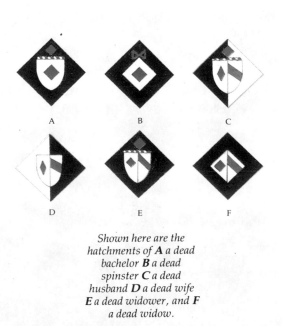

Shown here are the hatchments of **A** a dead bachelor **B** a dead spinster **C** a dead husband **D** a dead wife **E** a dead widower, and **F** a dead widow.

CHAPTER NINE

Ecclesiastical Heraldry

HERALDIC-LIKE devices have been used by churches since the beginning of Christianity. Ecclesiastical establishments have been granted land by the sovereign or, through piety or the desire to expiate sins, by landowners. Since the earliest times, therefore, they have had to fulfil the role of lord of the manor. Consequently, they have needed to use seals, badges and other devices to identify themselves and their retainers. These devices developed along Heraldic lines over the centuries and, although different denominations have different traditions, some general comments can be made.

EPISCOPAL HERALDRY

A bishop, who has authority over a number of priests in an area called a diocese, can, like the holder of a civic office, impale his personal arms, if he has them, with the official arms of his diocese. He places the diocesan arms on the dexter side of his shield and his own on the sinister side. On the Continent it is quite common for a bishop to quarter his arms with those of his see. He may also place a mitre over his shield and display behind it a crozier, or two in saltire, or an episcopal staff, as an emblem of his episcopal authority.

A number of terms in episcopal Heraldry deserve notice.

CROZIER This ceremonial staff, based on the shepherd's crook, symbolizes the episcopal authority of a bishop. It has a crook to gather in the lost, a stout staff to hold up the weak and a point to goad the reluctant!

EPISCOPAL HAT This is a flat hat with a wide brim, a shallow crown and pendant tassels. It is used in different colours and with different numbers of tassels to indicate the rank of the cleric.

EPISCOPAL STAFF This has a function similar to that of a crozier, but has a cross (of varying types) on the head instead of a crook.

Cardinals, who are of a higher rank than bishops, can display over their arms a red hat with tassels, fifteen on each side. If they are also bishops they can show under their hat a mitre and a crozier.

MITRES The mitre can take a variety of forms within two broad categories — completely plain, 'mitre simplex', or heavily decorated and jewelled, 'mitre preciosa'. Instead of displaying a mitre shown over his arms, a bishop may show a green episcopal hat with green tassels hanging down on both sides of the shield.

As a matter of style, the Catholic Church now favours an Achievement showing the episcopal arms with an ecclesiastical hat placed above and a staff placed behind. Anglican churches place a gold mitre and crossed croziers behind the arms. Eastern churches use the eastern forms of mitre and staff.

—— PAPAL HERALDRY ——

Popes, like other high dignitaries of the Church, have frequently used the horsehead-shaped shield, which looks less military and therefore is more suited to a man of God. For the same reason, it is not now felt appropriate for a cleric of any rank to display a crest and helm; hence the adoption of different orders of the clerical hat.

Papal heraldry has also adopted other symbols.

TIARA The tiara is the triple crown of the pope. The shape of the hat on which the three crowns are placed has long been considered an emblem of liberty and the three crowns are said to symbolize the pope's supremacy over the Church militant, the Church penitent and the Church triumphant. They also symbolize his three roles as priest, pastor and teacher.

CROSSED KEYS OF ST. PETER These are always shown with the tiara as a symbol of the papacy and are commonly placed on a red shield. A pope will place the tiara over the papal arms and the crossed keys behind his personal arms. The keys symbolize the power to bind or lock in and to set free or loose.

—— OTHER ECCLESIASTICAL —— SYMBOLS

UMBALINO OR PAVILION This is shown as an umbrella, or tent, with a red and gold striped cover. It is used as the emblem of a basilica in the Catholic Church.

With crossed keys it is used as the emblem of authority of the cardinal in charge ('Camerlengo') in an interregnum between popes. When placed with the cross keys behind, it has been used by Italian families in association with their arms to indicate that they have had a pope in the family.

PALLIUM This is a band of cloth, worn about the shoulders, charged with black crosses and two pendant strips. It is a symbol of authority given by the pope to an archbishop, who cannot commence his office until he receives it. It is displayed wherever it is possible to arrange it satisfactorily with the Achievement. It may be found as a charge on a shield, as it is in the Archdiocese of Canterbury.

ROSARY This string of beads, ten and one repeated five times, used to count repeated contemplative prayers, is sometimes found around a shield. It was used by a knight who had taken religious vows.

LEFT *The arms of a cardinal traditionally display the red cardinal's hat with 15 tassels on each side.*

BELOW LEFT *The arms of the Anglican Bishop of Ely: the gold mitre is in the Anglican style, but in this case there are no crossed croziers, which are usually displayed behind the arms.*

BELOW RIGHT *The arms of a bishop often display a green episcopal hat with tassels instead of a mitre.*

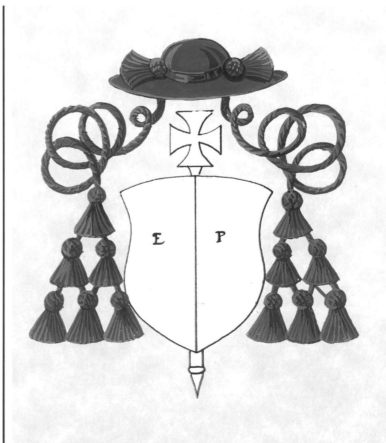

Orders of Chivalry and Entitlement to Arms

*I*T HAS long been the custom for sovereigns to instigate orders of chivalry to honour the nation's most distinguished men. These orders have emblems that the members wear and which appear on their Achievements. Practice varies widely from country to country and it is beyond the scope of this book to go into the subject in great detail.

CIRCLET European knights of an order often place a circlet around a shield. It is usually shown with a motto, as, for example, in the British Order of the Garter, which is blue with a gold edge and buckle and has the motto, 'Honi soit qui mal y pense'. — 'Evil be to he who evil thinks'.

CHAIN This is usually called a collar, a gold chain worn around the arms, with the emblems of the order in alternate links and the badge of the order pendant, as, for example, in the Swedish Order of the Seraphim. People may display collars of more than one order. Care should be taken with chains, as some officers of state also display a chain.

BADGE The badge of an order is displayed by lower-ranking members of the order on a riband, below the shield.

RELIGIOUS ORDERS OF CHIVALRY

These are survivors of the Crusades, when knights joined the military and hospital orders to fight for the Holy Lands and care for the sick and wounded soldiers and pilgrims. Some of these continue to exist for philanthropic purposes. They have their own arms and badges, known as crosses.

Grandmasters can show the arms of the order on their shields as a chief or quartering. Knights and dames of the order display the cross of their order behind the shield. Members can hang the cross of the order on a riband of the order below the shield.

ENTITLEMENT TO ARMS

Anyone may apply for a new grant of Arms, but a person is entitled to existing arms only if he can prove that he is descended in the male line from someone to whom a grant of arms had previously been made. Some countries permit people to assume arms at will, but there is then no guarantee that the arms are unique.

Heraldry is essentially a European phenomenon. Because Heraldic authorities in Europe have jurisdiction only over citizens of their own country, anyone wishing to enquire into their Heraldic status should of course apply to the authority in his own country.

In the New World the position is slightly different. Many of the peoples of those countries are of European stock. If a person wishes to prove his right to an existing Coat of Arms, he must apply to his country of origin or that of his ancestors. If he seeks a new Coat of Arms, he must apply to his own country. Heralds of one country cannot grant Coats of Arms to citizens of another, though they can make 'devisals of arms' to such people, which are then registered and recorded.

Modern Usage

THE variety of ways in which Heraldic bearings can be displayed, their decorative function and intriguing rules of form, have ensured the survival of this unique art form. The ownership of a Coat of Arms, whether it be one long in the family or one newly granted, is a matter of justified pride, a pride that can be expressed by displaying and using the arms in a wide variety of ways. Provided that they are employed with good taste, their use can only enhance the appearance of personal items and artefacts. Artists and craftsmen and some agencies specialize in supplying work of an Heraldic nature.

It is very important, when commissioning Heraldic work, to make sure that the artist is a competent exponent of Heraldic art who will render the work both artistically and correctly. Heraldry is not a representational art. The task of the Heraldic artist is to convey a brief message by using symbols. It is the symbolism of the items that he is trying to portray, not the actual item. He has to work with full regard to historical precedent and style, without forgetting that he is an artist of his own time.

It is worth going to a specialist agency which will be eager to meet both these ends and which will have on hand competent craftsmen who can undertake work in all kinds of media.

ON CHINA Painted and fired armorial painting and decoration.

ON CLOTH Painted, printed and sewn flags, banners and standards. Embroidered fire screens, stool and seat covers, chair backs. Painted and printed bedspreads. Sewn spinnaker sails for yachts. Heraldic costumes.

ON GLASS Engraved on table glass, doors and windows, table tops and firescreens. Stained-glass windows and hanging plaques. Lamp windows.

ON JEWELLERY Engraved rings, seals, personal items. Cast sculptured items, car mascots. Enamelled and jewelled cuff links, badges and brooches, pendants. Enamelled box lids and wall plaques.

ON LEATHER Embossed and gilded book bindings and covers, desk sets and chairbacks, boxes and belts.

ON PAPER AND VELLUM Paintings of Heraldic Achievements, illuminated and calligraphic illustrations, family trees, book plates in black and white and in full colour.

ON WOOD Wall plaques, carved, and gilded or painted. Carved newel posts, carved, painted and gilded backs and panels on furniture. Carved and painted or gilded shields.

Glossary

A

Abbess The senior member, or superior of a female religious house.

Abbey A building housing a society of monks or nuns. Also the society itself.

Abbot The senior member, or superior, of a male religious house.

Achievement of arms The complete assemblage of Heraldic accessories assigned to an individual, corporation or state.

Acorned Of the acorns of an oak, in separate specified colour.

Addorsed Of beasts or charges, back-to-back.

Affronty Of a *charge*, facing the observer.

Angled Of a *line of partition*, set at an angle.

Apaumy Of a hand or gauntlet, open to show the palm.

Arch (archy) Of a *line of partition*, in the form of an arch.

Argent The colour silver or white, a *tincture* of Heraldry; a *metal*.

Armed Of a human being or limb clothed in armour; the claws, beak, horns or tusks of a creature, in a separate, specified colour.

Armet A totally enclosed, close-fitting helmet with opening front.

Armiger A person entitled to bear arms.

Armorial A book listing *armorial bearings* alphabetically by the names of the bearers.

Armorial bearings The symbols born by an *armiger* his *coat armour*, *shield* and *banner* to distinguish him from others.

Artistic supporter *Supporter* with no Heraldic significance, added for effect.

Attributed arms *Armorial bearings* given to people who existed before Heraldry and to celestial and legendary figures.

Augmentation An additional charge or device awarded to an *armiger* as a reward for merit in some field or to commemorate a special event.

Azure The colour blue, a *tincture* of Heraldry.

B

Badge An Heraldic device belonging to an *armiger*, worn by his retainers and sympathizers.

Banner A square or rectangular flag upon which *armorial bearings* are displayed.

Bar A narrow strip on the *shield* in a horizontal plane ('barry', with several such strips).

Bars gemel Horizontal bars, arranged in pairs.

Basilisk An Heraldic monster, a reptile said to be hatched by a serpent from a cock's egg.

Bath, knights of the Active order of knights in Great Britain, in civil and military divisions.

Battled (embattled) Of a *line of partition*, having a crenellated edge like a battlement.

Baton A narrow, diagonal band not reaching the edge of the *shield*, in England sometimes in the form of the baton sinister, a mark of illegitimacy.

Beaked Of a beak, in a separate specified colour.

Belled With bells, attached to a hawk's leg for hawking, in a separate specified colour.

Bend A diagonal strip on the *shield* from *sinister* to *dexter* top; an *ordinary* 'per bend', divided in the same plane; 'In bend', charges placed in this plane.

Bend sinister A diagonal strip on the *shield* from *dexter* to *sinister* top.

Bendlet A narrow *bend*.

Bendy Covered with an even number of *bends*.

Bevelled Of a *line of partition*, broken so as to have two equally acute, alternate angles.

Bezant (byzant) A gold *roundle* representing a coin.

Bezanty Covered with gold coins.

Bicorporate Two bodies joined to one head.

Billet A rectangular shape, placed on end, representing a block of wood, usually used in large numbers to cover a *field*.

Billety Covered with billets.

Blazon The written description of *armorial bearings* 'to blazon' is to describe armorial bearings in words.

Bleu céleste The colour sky blue, a *tincture* of Heraldry.

Bonicon A mythical beast.

Bordure A narrow band around the edge of the *shield*.

Botony With ends like a clover leaf.

Bouget Two water carriers hanging from a yoke.

C

Caboshed Of a head, front-facing and cut off behind the ears.

Cadence The difference between the main bearer of arms in a family and cadet, or junior branches; a system of small additions and alterations to the *shield* to show this.

Caltrap (caltrop) A spiked device strewn on the ground to maim horses, used as a *charge*.

Calvary cross One of the forms of the cross, shown on three steps.

Canting *Armorial bearings* that in their concept and design include some reference or allusion to the name of the bearer.

Canton A square section, smaller than a *quartering* in the top dexter or sinister corner of the shield; a *sub-ordinary*.

Centaur A monster, half man and half horse.

Celestial crown An Heraldic *crown*.

Chain Separate links appearing as *charges*; sometimes a chain of office or of an order; when it is known as *collars*.

Chapeau A hat with a turned-up lining of *fur*, placed over the *helm* on which the *crest* stands; symbolic of especial dignity.

Charge Any device placed upon a *shield* or upon another item.

Chequey (checky) Of a *shield* or *charge*, covered all over with equal-sized squares, in two alternating colours, set in many rows.

Cherub The lowest order of the heavenly host; shown as a boy's face over two wings.

Chevalier A rank in French-speaking countries, equivalent to an English knight or German ritter.

Chevron A V-shaped strip, inverted, an *ordinary* ('Per chevron', the *field* or any area of colour divided as by a chevron).

Chevronels A bent bar on an escutcheon, half the breadth of the *chevron*; a small chevron.

Chief The top section of the *shield*; an *ordinary*; ('in chief', of *charges* placed in this area on a shield).

Cinquefoil A stylized flower, with five petals.

Circlet A riband placed around a *shield* bearing a motto, usually of one of the orders of knighthood.

Close Of a winged creature, when standing on the ground with its wings shut.

Coat armour A heavy, flowing, padded coat worn by knights to protect them from sword cuts, on which were painted their *armorial bearings*.

Coat of Arms A synonymous term for *coat armour*; now come to mean that which was painted on the coat, the *armorial bearings*. Because these are nowadays shown on a *shield*, a shield with armorial bearings painted on it is known as a Coat of Arms.

Cockatrice A mythological Heraldic monster, synonymous with a *basilisk*.

Coiled Of a snake, ready to strike.

Collar A chain of office of one of the orders of knighthood.

Collared Of a beast with a collar around its neck; synonymous with 'gorged'; not a chain of an order, unless specified.

College of arms The building in London where English Heralds have their chambers.

Colours The *tinctures* of Heraldry that represent red, blue, green, black and purple.

Combatant Two beasts or humans fighting each other.

Compartment A representation of the ground or whatever on which the *supporters*, *shield* and motto stand.

Compony Of a row of squares of two alternating colours, synonymous with 'gobony'. See *counter company* and *chequey*.

Coronel Crown-shaped tip of a lance, used in jousting to prevent injury.

Coronet A *metal*, decorated headwear, symbolic of rank.

Cotise A narrow band placed outside, and separate from, a wider band; can be found in multiples, specified; 'double cottice' should not be confused with *bar gemel*.

Couchant Of an animal, lying down with head erect.

Counter Opposite.

Counter-charged A *charge* placed upon a divided field with the *tinctures* reversed.

Counter-company Of two rows of differently coloured square sections arranged alternately.

Couped Of anything, cut off cleanly, for example an arm, head or branch.

Cowed Of a beast, with its tail between its legs.

Crescent A representation of the moon, shown with both horns upright (see also *increscent* and *decrescent*).

Crest A decorative accessory placed on the helmet.

Crested Of the *crest*, in a separate specified colour.

Crined With head-hair or mane, in a separate specified colour.

Cross 1 A horizontal and vertical band, each of the same colour, placed centrally on a *shield*; an *ordinary*; ('per cross', the *field* of the shield divided horizontally and vertically into four equal parts, synonymous with 'quarterly'; 'in cross', repeated *charges* placed upon a shield in a cross formation).
2 A charge on the shield representing a cross.

Crosslet A small cross with the end of each arm itself crossed.

Crown (heraldic) A symbolic *charge* used to denote an interest in a particular activity.

Crozier A ceremonial staff, symbolizing the role of a shepherd, used by a bishop.

Crusily Covered all over with little crosses.

Cubit arm An arm cut off cleanly between the hand and the elbow.

Cuffed Of the turned-up cuff of a sleeve, in its separate specified colour.

D

Dancy Of a *line of partition*, toothed or indented.

Decrescent Of a *crescent*, facing sinister.

Device An artistic, traditional or Heraldic symbol (or symbols) chosen to represent a person.

Devisal A unique design of *armorial bearings* devised and recorded by a Herald in one country for a citizen of another.

Dexter Right, considered from the point of view of the person bearing the *shield*, thus standing behind it.

Diapering A pattern in tone, on a plain *field*, to represent brocade; sometimes worked in gold paint.

Dimidiation The practice whereby half of one *Coat of Arms* is impaled (see impalement) on a shield with half of another Coat of Arms.

Diminutive Smaller, often multiple, version of an *ordinary* or *sub-ordinary*.

Disarmed Of a creature, without his beak, claws, teeth or tusks.

Displayed Of a winged creature, spread out on the *shield*.

Dormant Of a creature, asleep.

Double-arched Of a *line of partition*.

Double-queued Of a creature, with two tails.

Dovetailed Of a *line of partition*.

E

Elevated Of a bird with his wings out, the tips raised.

Emblazon To draw or paint a *Coat of Arms* in full colour.

Emblazoned Of a *Coat of Arms*, shown in pictorial form.

Enarched Of a *line of partition* having an arch in its inner angle.

Engrailed Of a *line of partition*, curvilinearly hotched.

Eradicated Of a plant or tree, pulled up, roots and all, from the ground.

Erased Of a limb of a human being or creature, or any part of an entity, as if pulled off the main body, leaving a jagged edge.

Erect Of any item, placed upright.

Ermine Of the *tinctures* of Heraldry, one of the *Furs*; white with black 'tails'.

Ermines Of the tinctures of Heraldry, one of the *Furs*; black with white 'tails'.

Erminois Of the tinctures of Heraldry, one of the *furs*; gold with black 'tails' (see *pean*).

Escarteled Of a *line of partition*, having square hotches.

Escutcheon A *shield*, usually small, used as a *charge* upon another.

Escutcheon of pretence A small *shield* bearing the arms of an heiress placed upon the shield of her husband's arms.

Estoil A representation of a star, with six wavy points or rays.

F

Face A creature's head *affronty* cut off cleanly behind the ears.

Falchion A broad-bladed, straight sword with one side curved.

Feather One of the coverings of a bird, used as a *charge* and *crest*.

Fetterlock A removable shackle around the feet of a creature or person.

Fesse A horizontal strip across the middle of the *shield*; an *ordinary*; ('per fesse', the *field* divided horizontally into two equal parts; 'in fess', *charges* placed on the shield in this position).

Fesse-wise *Charges* placed in a horizontal plane.

Fesse-point The mid-point of *shield*.

Field The colour that the *shield* is painted before anything is placed upon it, and the divisions of this, if more than one *tincture* is used.

Fimbriated Of a *charge* with a strong outline of a different *tincture*.

Fitchy With a point, so that it can be stuck in the ground, especially of a cross.

Flaunches Two semi-circular sections on the sides of a *shield*, of a different *tincture* from the *field*.

Fleur de lis A stylized form, in many varieties, of the lily.

Fleuretty Of a cross, from the ends issuing in *fleurs de lis*.

Flory (fleury) 1. With the ends terminating in *fleurs de lis*.
2. Of a *line of partition* decorated thus.

Formy Of a cross made with wide triangular pieces, meeting at the centre.

Fountain A *roundle* with white and blue wavy lines.

Fraise (frase, fraze) A white *cinquefoil* representing the strawberry flower, from the French, *fraise*.

Fret Two diagonal strips interlacing a void diamond shape, said to represent the knot of a fishing net.

Fretty Covered with interwoven diagonal lines from both directions.

Fructed Of the fruit a plant or tree, in separate specified colour.

Fusil An elongated diamond shape.

Furs The *tinctures* in Heraldry that represent fur.

G

Garb A sheaf of wheat or other grain-bearing plant; also applied to arrows or anything else shown in bundles.

Garter, the A blue garter, worn below the knee, bearing the motto, 'Honi soit qui mal y pense', 'Evil be to he who evil thinks,' by Knights of the Garter; also displayed around their shields.

Garter, Order of The oldest and senior order of knighthood still existing in England.

Gentleman An untitled person entitled to bear arms.

Glade A spear with serrated inner edges for catching eels and other fish.

Gobony See *compony*.

Golpe A mulberry-coloured *roundle*, representing a wound.

Gonfanon A long flag, suspended from the top and hanging vertically having long tails.

Gorged See *collared*.

Goutte (gutte) A small, drop-shaped figure of specified *tincture*, used as a *charge*.

Goutty Covered with small, drop-shaped figures.

Grady Of a *line of partition*, stepped.

Grant of arms A Formal document giving sole right to a person and his heirs to bear arms, granted by a competent authority.

Griffin (gryphon) A mythical beast, having the head and wings of an eagle and the body and hind quarters of a lion.

Guardant Of a creature or human, looking out of the *shield* at the observer.

Gules Of the *tinctures* of Heraldry, the colour red.

Gunstone A black *roundle*, also known as a *pellate*.

Gyron A wedge-shaped *charge*, placed in the lower diagonal half of a *canton*.

Gyrony Of wedge-shaped sections, formed by diagonal, vertical and horizontal lines, crossing in the centre.

H

Habited Of clothes, with a specified colour or type; synonymous with 'vested'.

Hand of Ulster A red hand, palm showing, on a white *shield*, the *badge* of a baronet.

Harpy A monster, having a woman's face and body and a bird's wings and claws.

Hart A full-grown red deer stag.

Hatchment A diamond-shaped board with *armorial bearings* painted for the funeral of the bearer.

Haurient Of a fish, swimming to the top of the *shield*.

Hawking Favourite sport of the Middle Ages, in which a trained bird of prey was used to catch game.

Heater A shape of *shield*, resembling a flat iron.

Helm Heraldic term for a helmet.

Horned With horns, in a separate specified colour.

I

Impalement The practice of placing two, sometimes three, *Coats of Arms* side by side on the same shield.

Incensed Issuing flames or vapour.

Increscent Of a *crescent*, facing *dexter*.

Indented Of a *line of partition*, having a series of similar indentations or notches.

Infula Ribands hanging from the back of the papal *tiara* or a bishop's mitre; derived originally from a long band tied around the head and hanging down the back.

Invected (invecked) Of a *line of partition*, having a series of small convex lobes.

Inverted Of a winged creature, with the wings open, the tips downward.

Issuant Of a *charge*, when it comes out of another underneath it, or from off the borders of the *shield*.

J

Jessant de lis Of a face, placed before a *fleur de lis* with the lower part of the fleur thrust out through the mouth.

Jessed Of the jesses trying a bell to a falcon's leg, in a separate specified colour.

Jousting Organized combat between mounted knights for pageantry, display, prowess and training.

K

King of arms The senior Herald in a country.

Knight One elevated to this rank and admitted to one of the orders of knighthood by the competent authority in recognition of deeds of valour or great service; a non-hereditary rank; 'Ritter' in Germany, 'chevalier' in France.

Knot Loops of interlaced cord frequently used as *badges* or *charges*.

L

Label A strip across the top section of the *shield*, with pendant tabs; usually a sign of a son, by common usage the heir.

Lambrequin Synonymous with *mantelling*.

Langued Of the tongue, in a separate specified colour.

Leaved Of the leaves of a plant, in a separate colour.

Ledger stone A memorial slab placed in the floor of a church.

Line of partition See *partition*. Lines drawn to delineate divisions and *charges* can be of many different configurations.

Lioncel A small lion, used to describe one of many on one *shield*.

Livery The uniform worn by a lord's retainers, bearing his colours.

Livery company Originally a medieval trade guild, nowadays involved in charitable works.

Lodged Of a deer, lying down.

Lozenge A diamond-shaped piece. See also *mascule* and *rustre*.

Lozengy Of an all-over lozenge pattern, made by crossing diagonal lines.

Lymphad A small sailing vessel, with one sail, sometimes furled, and sometimes with oars.

M

Mace (Battle) A spiked iron ball on a shaft, wielded in the hand, the ball sometimes attached by a short length of chain.
(Ceremonial) A large ornamental item, often with an orb and crown on top as symbol of civic authority.

Mantelling A short cloth attached to the back of the helmet to keep off the sun's heat and protect against sword cuts.

Mandrake A human monster, formed from the root of the plant of the same name.

Marshalling The practice of combining two or more Coats of Arms on a *shield* or in one *Achievement*.

Martlet A bird of the swift order, shown with no feet.

Mascule A *lozenge*-shaped figure, voided in the centre. See also *rustre*.

Maunch Representation of a sleeve, with a long pendant pocket from the wrist.

Melusine A human, female monster, with two fish tails.

Mermaid A human, female monster with a fish tail.

Merman A human, male monster with a fish tail.

Metal Of the *tinctures* of Heraldry, the colours that represent silver and gold.

Mill-rind Iron bracket to take the spindle in the centre of a millstone to prevent wear.

Moline One of the forms of the cross, the arms terminating in curved branches resembling the ends of a *mill-rind*.

Mollet (mullet) A five-pointed *star* shape, not to be confused with a star (see *estoil*); when pierced representing a *spur rowel*.

Moon Shown either full, with a human face, to differentiate it from a *plate* or as a *crescent*. See also *increscent* and *decrescent*.

Mural An Heraldic *crown*, in embattled form.

Murrey One of the *tinctures* of Heraldry, a purple or red *stain*.

N

Naiant Of fish, swimming across the *shield*, heads to the dexter.

National arms *Armorial bearings* used by countries, expressing territorial allegiance.

Naval crown One of the Heraldic crowns.

Navel point The lower middle point of a *shield*, below the *fessee point*.

Nebuly Of a *line of partition*, of a wavy or serpentine form.

Nowed Knotted, of a rope, a tail, a snake etc.

O

Octofoil A flower with eight petals.

Ogress A black *roundle*, synonymous with *gunstone*.

Opinicus An Heraldic beast, the same as the griffin, but with *four* lion's legs.

Or Of the *tinctures* representing *metals*, the colour gold.

Ordinary The principal geometric *charge* on a *shield*.

Ordinary of arms A book listing *armorial bearings* alphabetically according to the principal *charges*, so that the bearers of arms can be ascertained by reference to the description.

Orle A narrow band on the *shield*, following its shape, but set in from the edge; ('in orle', *charges* placed upon a shield in the disposition of an orle).

Ounce A mythical beast resembling a leopard, in Heraldry often a black panther.

Overall Of a *charge* placed on a *shield* on top of whatever is on the shield already.

P

Pairle A division of the *field* into three radiant sections.

Pale An *ordinary*, being a vertical stripe or band in the middle of the *shield*; ('in pale' *charges* placed in a vertical alignment on the shield; 'per pale', one of the divisions of the field).

Palewise Of *charges* placed on the *shield* vertically.

Palisado An Heraldic *crown*, resembling a palisade.

Pall A Y-shaped band, in three ships, placed upon a *shield*, derived from the *pallium*.

Pallet A very narrow *pale*.

Pallium A narrow, ring-like band of cloth lying over the shoulders, symbolizing the authority of an archbishop.

Paly Of the *field*, divided into an equal number of vertical strips.

Paly bendy Of the *field*, divided into sections by vertical and diagonal lines.

Paper heraldry Derogatory term applied to Heraldic accessories designed after the practical function of heraldry had passed, which could never have been used for their apparent purpose.

Passant Of a creature, walking across the *shield*.

Passion cross One of the forms of the cross; the standard crucifix.

Patonce One of the forms of the cross, having its arms extending in a curved form from the centre.

Patriarchial cross One of the forms of the cross, having two transverse arms, the upper one being the shorter.

Pavilion A figure in the shape of a tent, or umbrella, used as a *charge*; especially in ecclesiastical Heraldry; also called an 'umbrellino'.

Pean One of the Heraldic *tinctures* that represent the *furs*, black with gold spots.

PEGASUS A horse monster, having wings.
PELLATE A black *roundle*, synonymous with *ogress* and *gunstone*.
PELLATY Covered with pellates.
PENNED See *guilled*.
PENNON A small pointed flag fixed at the lance point.
PEON A broad arrowhead, the inside edge serrated.
PHOENIX A mythical bird.
PIERCED Of a *charge* with a hole in it through which can be seen the colour of whatever lies underneath, unless otherwise specified.
PILE A triangular piece from the top of the *shield*, point towards the bottom.
PILE BENDY A horizontal pile, with its base to *sinister*, its point to *dexter*.
PILGRIM STAFF A staff with a hook near the top to carry a pilgrim's bag.
PLATE A *roundle*, silver or white.
PLATY Covered with *plates*.
POMMEL One of the forms of the cross in which each arm terminates in a roundle.
POMME A green *roundle*, representing an apple.
PORTCULLIS A defensive grid dropped down in a doorway to keep out intruders.
POTENT One of the tinctures representing the *furs*, formed of or terminating in crutch-heads.
POTENT One of the forms of the cross, the arms terminating in potents, or crutch-heads.
POTENTY Of a *line of partition*, formed by a series of potents, or crutch heads.
POWDERED Covered all over with small *charges*.
PRIDE, IN HIS A bird such as a peacock or turkey with his tail spread is said to be 'in his pride'.
PROFILE Of a human face, facing the *dexter*.
PROPER Of anything in Heraldry *blazoned* in its natural colour.
PURPURE Of the *tinctures* of Heraldry, purple.

— Q —

QUARTER The top dexter quarter on a *shield*.
QUARTERING One of any number of divisions on a shield, on which are placed different *Coats of Arms*.
QUARTER-PIERCED Of a cross form on the *shield*, the centre removed to show the colour of the *field*, so that all the remaining cross-sections and all the field sections are as near equal as possible.
QUATREFOIL A stylized flower with four petals, representing the poppy.
QUEUE FOURCHY Of the forked tail of a creature.
QUILLED Of the shaft of a feather, synonymous with 'penned'.

— R —

RAGULY A *line of partition*, having alternate projections and depressions like a battlement, but set obliquely.
RAMPANT Of a creature, reared up to fight.
RAYONNÉ A *line of partition*, having alternating pointed projections and depressions with wavy edges.

REFLEXED Of a lead or chain on a creature, bent over the back and down to the ground.
REGUARDANT Of a creature or human, looking backwards, over the shoulder.
RESPECTANT Of two creatures or humans, looking at each other.
REVERSED Of a weapon or tool, upside down, with the point downwards.
ROMPU (ROMPEE) Broken, of an *ordinary* or *sub-ordinary*.
ROSE EN SOLEIL An Heraldic rose charged upon a *sun in splendour*. q.v.
ROUNDLE A circle, of various colours, each having its own name.
ROWEL The star-shaped object on the end of a spur.
ROYAL A full-grown red deer stag, synonymous with 'hart'.
RUSTRE A diamond-shaped figure with a hole in the middle. See *mascule* and *lozenge*.

— S —

SABLE Of the Heraldic *tinctures*, the colour black.
SAGITTARIUS A *charge* representing *sagittary*, often with a drawn bow.
SAGITTARY A human monster, having the body of a lion joined to the torso of a man.
SALAMANDER A mythical creature, lizard-like and supposed to be able to endure fire.
SALIENT Of a creature, leaping.
SALTIRE an ordinary, two crossed strips across the *shield*, diagonally, ('per saltire', the *field* divided in four parts, diagonally; 'in saltire' of charges set upon the shield in the plane of a saltire).
SANGUINE Of the *tinctures* of Heraldry one of the *stains*, dark blood-red.
SEAL A tool with an Heraldic device carved upon it, used to make an impression in wax, as a sign of authenticity; the wax impression itself.
SEAX A curved, broad-bladed sword with a notch cut in the back.
SAXON CROWN An Heraldic *crown*.
SEEDED Of a flower, denoting the colour of the centre of the flower; also of a pod, where the seeds show.
SEGREANT Of a griffin, as *rampant* is of a lion reared up to fight.
SEJANT Of a beast, sitting upright facing *dexter*.
SEMY (SEMEE) Covered all over with small *charges*.
SEMEE DE LIS Covered all over with *fleurs de lis*.
SERAPHIM The first order of the angelic host.
SHAKEFORK A Y-shaped *charge*, similar to a *pall* which does not reach to the edge of a *shield*.
SHAMROCK The three-leafed plant emblematic of Ireland; as a *charge*, shown *slipped*, with heart-shaped petals.
SHEAF A bundle of arrows, reeds, spears, synonymous with *garb*.
SHIELD The main defensive item of a man fighting on foot or horseback, used to ward off offensive blows. Nowadays the main item on which to display *armorial bearings*.
SINISTER Left, considered from the point of view of the person bearing the *shield*, thus standing behind it.

SINOPLE Of the *tinctures* of Heraldry, the colour green in French usage.
SLIPPED Of a plant or flower, with a stem.
SOARING Of a winged creature, facing the front and flying with both wings outstretched.
SPHINX A mythical beast, usually represented as having the head of a woman and the (winged) body of a lion.
SPUR ROWEL A star-shaped spike placed on a spur, synonymous in Heraldry with a pierced *mollet*.
STAINS Colours of the *tinctures* of Heraldry that are not primary colours.
STALL PLATE Some of the orders of knighthood have their own chapels, in which members of the order display their armorial banners, each over his own seat, or stall. Past and deceased occupiers of a stall, whose banners have been taken down, have a metal, enamelled plate of their Achievement affixed to the stall.
STATANT Of a creature, simply standing, facing the *dexter*.
STANDARD A long flag with a partly-coloured fringe, now displaying the arms, *crest*, motto and *livery colours* of the bearer.
STAR In Heraldry represented as a figure with six wavy arms, called an *Estoil*; with five points it is called a *mollet*.
SUB-ORDINARY Any one of a group of the smaller, less frequently used, geometric shapes found as *charges*.
SUNBURST A cloud with the sun's rays *issuant*.
SUN IN SPLENDOUR The sun, issuing rays.
SUPPORTER Any creature holding up a shield or helm, most commonly in pairs.

— T —

TABARD A loose smock, without sleeves, on which *armorial bearings* are sometimes *emblazoned*.
TALBOT A large hunting dog with drooping ears, the model for representations of a hunting dog in Heraldry.
TARGET A *shield*, so named because it was at the shield that knights aimed their assaults during a *tournament*; usually of a small ceremonial sort, carried at a funeral; often abbreviated to 'targ'.
TAU A cross in the shape of a 'T', from that letter in the Greek Alphabet; known as a St. Anthony's Cross.
TENNÉ (TENNY) Of the *tinctures* of Heraldry, one of the *stains*, tawny orange.
TIARA Usually refers, in Heraldry, to the papal headpiece of three *crowns*.
TINCTURE In Heraldry the term for all the colours employed.
TILTING SPEAR Special spear used in *tournaments*.
TOMB EFFIGY A prone statue of the deceased placed upon his tomb.
TORSE A twist of material covering the joint between *crest* and *helm*, synonymous with 'wreath'.
TORTEAU A red roundle representing a cake of bread.

TRESSURE A narrow band placed on a *shield*, following its shape, but not touching the edge; usually found as a double tressure of two such bands; the two bands of a double tressure being a little wider than the one band of an *orle*.
TRANSFIXED Pierced by a weapon.
TRICK A shorthand way of nothing down a *blazon*.
TRICORPORATE Of a creature, having one head and three bodies.
TRIPLE-TOWERED A castle or tower with three smaller towers on top.
TRIPPANT (TRIPPING) Of deer, trotting or walking across the *shield* to the *dexter*, with one paw raised.
TUFTED Of creatures, having tufts of hair on their knees, elbows, flanks, shoulders or chin.
TUDOR ROSE An Heraldic rose, composed of a white rose charged upon a red rose, reversed, if placed upon a red field; occasionally found *quartered* and *counter-charged*, plain quartered or parted per *pale*.
TYGER An Heraldic creature, bearing little resemblance to a real tiger.

— U —

UNDY Of a *line of partition*, wavy.
UNGULED Of the hoofs of a creature, in a separate specified colour.
UNICORN Fabulous horse monster with horn.
URCHIN A hedgehog.
URDY Of a *line of partition*, pointing, having points.
URIANT Of a fish, swimming down to the bottom of the *shield*.
UMBRELLINO See *pavilion*.

— V —

VAIR Of the *tinctures* in Heraldry, one of the furs, (blue and white).
VAIRY Of a *field* of the *vair* type, but of specified *tincture*.
VALLARY CROWN An Heraldic *crown*; (from the Roman tradition of bestowing a crown on the first to mount an enemy's rampart).
VAMBRACED Of an arm, protected by armour.
VERT Of the *tinctures* of Heraldry, one of the *colours*, green.
VESTED See *habited*.
VISOR The opening front of a helmet.
VOIDED Of a *charge*, appearing in outline only.
VOLANT Of a bird, flying across the *shield* with wings expanded.
VULNED Wounded and bleeding.

— W —

WATTLED Of a cock or other fowl, with skin hanging from the chin.
WAVY Of *lines of partition*.
WOODWOSE (WOODHOUSE) A wild man of the woods, used as a *charge* and sometimes as a *supporter*.
WREATH See *torse*.
WREATHY Of a *subordinary*, depicted as if made like a wreath, with twists of cloth of various colours.
WYVERN (WIVERN) A mythical beast, being a winged dragon with two eagle-like feet and a barbed, serpentine tail.

— Y —

YALE An Heraldic beast with horns and tusks.

Index

Picture Credits

The British Library: pp 14 top, 16, 17.
Clive Hicks: pp 7, 10 top left, 11, 14 bottom, 32 top, 43 right, 46, 48, 54, 55 right, 59, 63 bottom.
Cognizance Heraldic Artwork Agency: pp 11 top right, 17 top, 32 centre and below, 37, 40, 41, 42, 50, 55 top left, 56 right, 57.
E T Archive: pp 10, 15, 18, 19, 21, 23, 24, 26, 30, 34, 44, 51, 60.
A F Kersting: pp 8, 9, 39, 52, 56 left, 61, 62, 63 top.
Wooden carving, illustrated on page 40, by Derek Riley. Moulded shields, illustrated on pages 50 and 55, by de Havilland and Howell.

Acknowledgements

The author wishes to thank Marie Neal for her untiring and patient help in preparing this book, and the Cognizance Heraldic Artwork Agency for permission to reproduce photographs of the work of contemporary heraldic craftsmen. Thanks are also due to all those who have offered help and criticism, and to Lorraine Greenoak who precipitated the whole project.